Also by Steven LaChance
The Uninvited
Blessed are the Wicked
Crazy: A Prayer for the Dead

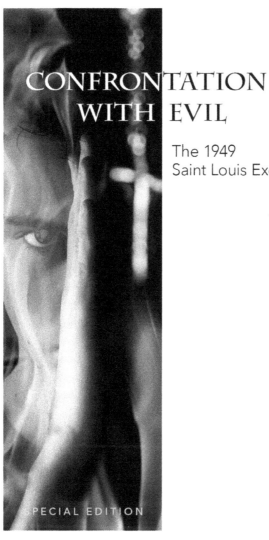

CONFRONTATION WITH EVIL

The 1949
Saint Louis Exorcism

SPECIAL EDITION

To Roland Doe, wherever you may be today, this is for you because it is clear that you were a victim in many different ways. My deepest thank you, my prayers, and my gratitude will always be with you—in this life and in the next.

Introduction

Contents

Appendix

References

On [SAT.] February 26, 1949, there appeared to be scratches on the boy's body for about four successive nights. After the fourth night words were written in printed form. These letters were clear but seemed to have been scratched on the body by claws.

Since Mrs. XXXXXXXX is a native St. Louisan, she thought of leaving her home and taking the boy to St. Louis in order to avoid some of these strange manifestations. It seems that whatever force was writing the words was in favor of making the trip to St. Louis. On one evening the word "Louis" was written on the boy's ribs in deep red.

—From Father Raymond Bishop's diary, 1949

Introduction

Growling filled the house as the priest, standing at the opposite end of the hallway, kissed his purple stole and placed it around his neck. Anticipation of what lay ahead filled the priest with not only dread but also a clear sense of anger. The demon from the room down the hall began to scream as the priest brought his crucifix to his lips to kiss the sacrament. "Your God is dead, Priest, he is not going to help you," the demon's voice filled the entire house with its vile speech. Bible, crucifix, holy water, and liturgical vestments—the priest was now completely armored and dressed for the long battle that was ahead for himself and the young boy who laid behind the door at the end of the hall, writhing in pain as he wrestled with the demon within him.

The priest began the long walk down the hallway toward the boy's door, which now appeared to the priest to be moving in and out with the loud breathing of the demon within the boy. Whispers began to fill the hallway as he walked slowly, "Fuck the priest. Bend him over and fuck him." Suddenly the hall began to shake violently, almost knocking the priest off of his feet with a vicious rumble. A loud giggle from behind the breathing door at the end of the hall continued its demonic taunt - meant to create fear in the faithful.

The priest could see one of the hinges on the door begin to give way as he reached out to turn the doorknob. The door instantly blew off its frame with violent force, throwing the priest to the floor. The priest covered his head with his arms to protect himself. He stumbled to his feet, grasping the crucifix tightly within his hand with resolve, and he peered into the room.

The boy lay tied to the bed. His face was ashen in color with blood and ooze running from cuts all over his body, including the ashen face. The priest worked to avoid gazing into the glare of the glowing yellow serpentine eyes of the possessed teenage boy. "Enter if you dare, Priest," the boy spoke with a low, guttural, and almost animal-like growl.

"Cut! Will someone get this damn lighting fixed on the boy. It's supposed to show the shadows on the damn wall," the director of the horror film barked at the crew. "Can I get a drink over here," the boy in the bed said, breaking character because he was thirsty.

This scene has been played out over and over again throughout the years in many horror films. It is always displayed with over-the-top theatrical special effects, and rarely is it ever done with any care to realism. It is nothing more than an entertaining version of diabolic demonic possession. The lack of realism, the focus on the spinning heads and flowing pea soup has lessened the reality of what true possession is and how it works. Horror films are not only guilty of their misrepresentation, but within the past decade, supposed reality television has fed audiences a steady dose of the fantastical demonic while telling its audiences what they are about to see is real and unscripted. The reality of reality television is that it is completely scripted and much of what you see is not real—it is either faked or completely and absolutely overdramatized.

So what is the truth about demonic possession and why is there this somewhat misguided attraction to it? Well, that would be the question, wouldn't it? If you are expecting a rehash of the same kind of demonic theatrics that has characterized the film industry throughout the years, then you are going to be somewhat disappointed. However, if you want the truth about possession and how it works, then you are more than welcome to come on this journey with me.

The best way to start any journey is with a personal introduction. Many of you may have never read a single word I have written before, and for some of you, it may have been some time since you read one of my other works. So I think an introduction might be the best way to begin. My name is Steven LaChance. By all records and understanding, the paranormal was not something that I stepped into lightly. I was thrown into it headfirst, and down the rabbit hole I went. In May of 2001, I moved into a house in Union, Missouri, which turned out to be home to one of the most violent hauntings in paranormal history. The Roman Catholic Church, in a 156-page report, labeled "The Screaming House Haunting," a demonic infestation that eventually led to oppression, obsession, and finally, possession.

For the past eleven years I have helped other families and individuals in paranormal need. I am known for my work and research within the paranormal. Because of my ability to find new locations, dissect research, and propose theories about old locations, some have referred to me as a paranormal pioneer. I have been responsible for bringing some of the most prolific paranormal locations to the forefront, including the Screaming House, Zombie Road, Morse Mill Hotel, the Pythian Castle, Tri-County Truck Stop and many more.

My personal research and investigation into the famous 1949 Exorcism Case has not only turned heads but has provided new insights on the events that took place during and after the 1949 exorcism. The 1949 Exorcism Case was the inspiration for William Peter Blatty's novel, The Exorcist, published in 1971. From there the book spawned the cult classic film, The Exorcist, which haunted audiences nationwide in 1973. This book starts with a quote from the infamous diary of Father Bishop, one of the clergy assigned to the case. We will be delving deeper into that diary a little later in this book.

I was born in St. Louis, Missouri. I spent the first five years of my life living within the city. The smell of the hops from the brewery will at any moment bring back my childhood memories. It was much later in life that I learned the first house I lived in as a boy in St. Louis was actually haunted. I moved to the small rural town of Washington, Missouri when I was twelve years old, leaving behind the city I have always loved. I moved back to St. Louis for a short time in the nineties but found myself right back in Washington where my parents were living. I was extremely bitter about this move and I longed to return to the city I loved. I ended up in Union, Missouri, which is the next town over from Washington. That is where the infamous Screaming House Haunting occurred.

It was March of 2014 and I was ready to move back to St. Louis. My children were grown and it was finally time to start doing some things for myself again, which meant moving back to St. Louis. The search for a house began and it continued until we pulled up to the curb in front of a house sitting on top of a hill. I got out of the car to greet Kimberly DeLapp, my real estate agent. She stood proudly looking at the house on the hill. As I followed her proud gaze to the house on the hill, I looked around the neighborhood and realized, "Oh my God, this is the neighborhood of the Exorcism Case and this house looks like the Amityville Horror house." Kim turned to me and gave me a perplexed look. "This is going to be the perfect home for you, Steven, I can feel it," she said with confidence.

Kimberly DeLapp was one of the top real estate agents in St. Louis. She did the work because she loved helping people find their homes. It was her thing and she took her job very seriously. Anyone who was lucky and honored enough to work with Kim always ended up in the right home. At this moment I had to put my faith in that. We had already looked at about six houses that day, but that was the first house where I saw Kim light up like that. She was always the first to say, "I don't think this is the right place for you." For Kim, the right place meant something. For the first time she was saying that the house at the top of the hill was the right place, so I followed her up to the front steps.

The very first thing I noticed while walking under the arches to the front porch was the black-and-white mosaic tile that made up the front porch. It was in perfect condition. The front door was made of mostly glass and revealed the view of the entryway. "Oh wow Kim! Are those the original wood floors?" Before my eyes was a historic, three bedroom home with a roomy living room, kitchen, and dining room. The winding staircase was open and bright. The ceilings were exceptionally high, which was a huge selling point for my son Mathew, who is six foot ten.

About halfway through the walk-through, Kim grabbed me by the arm and said, "Steven, I can see you living here. This is the perfect place for you! Trust me, I know." It was exactly what I told her I wanted in my dream house: all brick, front porch, an office, wood floors, renovated with preservation in mind, and a backyard. It was the kind of house I always had seen myself living in, and for some strange reason, I could feel in the pit of my stomach that this was it - this was going to be my home.

I bought the house on May 1, 2014, and the move was exhausting. It is never easy packing your life up and moving from one place to another. But the truth is, it was not even close to easy. First, the truck we originally rented was a one-way rental, which meant I was scrambling at the last moment to find one that wasn't. After finally getting the truck situation figured out, we began packing our lives into a rental. It took an hour to drive from the old house to the new one. My cat, Zeke, slept quietly in his carrier at my feet as my son Matthew, now driving the truck, waved to his friends Frog and Cody as they passed us honking their horn. Both were helping us with the move.

The hour trip seemed too long and drawn out. It was a relief when we pulled up behind Frog in front of the house. We finally made it and we were there. I was looking at boxes everywhere and thinking it was going to be a long time before anything began to feel normal again. "I have the beds set up." Matthew was calling to me from upstairs with a voice that would wake the dead. Let's hope there were no dead here to wake. I have to admit that has always been a fear of mine. The house is a hundred years old, and no matter what people were saying to me, it felt like I was rolling the dice here. My cat, Zeke, seemed to be very happy with his new surroundings though. He kept running up and down the stairs. He loved sitting in the windowsill on the stairway and looking out upon his new world. Well, if Zeke could relax, maybe I should relax as well.

I am sitting here right now writing this in the same neighborhood where the 1949 exorcism of a young boy, which inspired The Exorcist, took place. It is a story that has been reiterated time and time again. The problem with the telling is simply that it's nothing more than a reiteration. To me, the case has always contained more questions than answers. I am going to turn my gift of discernment toward this case and finally attempt to answer the questions that should have been answered many years ago. What really happened, and why has this case fascinated generations of people? I am not going to shy away from the controversy surrounding this case. If you thought you knew everything you needed to know about the 1949 Exorcism Case, you may be surprised by what you actually don't know or haven't considered, especially where this case is located. If you have never heard of the 1949 Exorcism Case, then get ready to have everything you think to be true, challenged.

So turn on a few lights in the house if you are reading this at night. Be aware of your surroundings and what is behind you at all times. We are going to roll up our sleeves and dive deeper into this case than anyone has ever dared. I have called upon my guardian angel for protection. I hope you have called upon yours.

St. Anthony of Paduah Catholic Church

Saint Louis, Missouri

Chapter 1
Where the Devil Played

      This new adventure began in a seemingly innocent way as I found myself standing in front of a Catholic Church courtyard just up the street from my new home. Mathew and I were both stunned when we approached the statue located in the church courtyard. Directly in front of us stood a statue of St. Anthony holding a baby in his arms, but St. Anthony's head was missing. There could have almost been a soundtrack from a film like *The Omen* playing in the background. Something creepy on the lines of "Requiem" would have been perfect. Matthew whispered to me quietly, "Why do you suppose he is missing his head?" You could tell by the look on his face that he was more than a little puzzled by the scene. "I have no clue, but I know I am getting a picture of this." I laughed as I pulled my cell phone out of my pocket and started taking pictures. Matthew stepped back because he knew there was no stopping me once I set my mind on something. Cars were slowing down behind us on the street to look at what was of so much interest. "Hurry up and finish, Pops. People are looking at us like we are crazy." I'm not sure why a twenty-something would find his father taking a picture embarrassing, but the source of the embarrassment was probably coming from what his father was taking a picture of. Regardless of which point of view he held at the time, I knew I wasn't going to miss this shot for the world.

Sitting on the front porch after returning home, I looked at the picture on my phone and wondered to myself why someone would take the head from a religious statue. Now you could say maybe this person just decided it would be funny to decapitate St. Anthony. You could also say that maybe they were a weird collector of such strange and exotic items. It reminded me of William Peter Blatty's book, *Legion*. In this book, the Gemini Killer, who had possessed a priest, replaces the heads of his victims with the heads of religious statues. It was such a bizarre coincidence. Here I was, sitting in the neighborhood of the famed Exorcism Case, and headless religious statues were adorning nearby churches. Most have heard of the 1949 Exorcism Case, but not many realize that most of it happened in the neighbor- hood I live in. There is a tremendous amount of information and misinformation out there about this particular case. Everyone wants to know how the boy became possessed and why the demon chose him as a conduit. Most paranormal researchers and demonologists would look to the stages of demonic possession for the literal answer.

The first stage of demonic possession is obsession, according to *The Encyclopedia of Demons and Demonology* (Guiley 2009). The word obsession comes from the Latin *obsidere*, which refers to a state of siege or an attack on a person or personality from within by demons.

The next stage is infestation, which is the "presence of demons in a place, object, or animal.

Infestation occurs when demons are able to take up residence and create disturbances. It is a precursor to more serious demonic problems, such as oppression and possession."

Infestation can be the result of people's curses, magic spells, rituals or even actions. The Catholic Church teaches that using Ouija boards, making a pact with the devil or leading a sinful life can cause an infestation. "Infesting demons create chaos and fear through poltergeist-like activity, the manifestation of shadowy figures and other paranormal phenomena. Victims may hear knocks on the door when no one is present." Knocks mocking the Trinity that occur in threes or sixes (double three), scratching sounds on doors or in walls, hot or cold spots, pounding on the walls or roof, plumbing that does not turn off, and levitation of small objects are all signs of infestation. Infestations can be subtle, with demons creeping in quietly to gain more influence over the victim.

The next stage is oppression, which is the demonic influence that takes control of a victim's will. This type of tormenting can lead to an internal or psychological breakdown. Oppressed victims are terrorized by demonic screams, heavy breathing, footsteps, knockings, hellish moans and inhuman voices, nightmares and disturbed sleep, and disgusting smells, such as sulfur or rotting flesh. Levitation of people or large objects and furniture and, finally, materializations of a black form that personifies evil are the culmination of this oppression caused by the demon. Because of the demon, the victims believe they are insane. Dramatic personality changes are accompanied by mood swings and depression. The victim will make heavy use of foul or obscene language. Friends and family feel the victim has undergone a marked personality change. This stage can be relieved by the Rite of Exorcism, accompanied by the spiritual reform of the victim.

Demonic possession is the final stage. Demonic possession is complete when a demon inhabits a person's body and controls their thoughts, words, and actions. "A possessed person can seem normal for periods of time and then exhibit bizarre uncontrolled behavior attributed to the demon. During the demonic episodes, the victim is entranced, and when they end, there is no transition period of a return to normalcy." Victims that are possessed are usually possessed by more than one demon, and unless they are exorcised, the demons can lead to deterioration of health, death or suicide.

Most of the time people do not discuss obsession, so you might find it interesting that it is included here, but there needs to be some accuracy when discussing these things. Many times people will include obsession with oppression, but they are very different things. Symptoms of obsession often include sudden ongoing attacks or obsessive thoughts that are sometimes irrational and so powerful that the victim is unable to free themselves. The obsessed person lives in a perpetual state of desperation and depression, and attempts at suicide can often occur. Obsession almost always influences dreaming and you will hear the obsessed talk about these very real, lucid dreams.
Those of you who know me know that I took a personal journey through all of these steps, and let me say, diabolical obsession is not pleasant or desirable by any means. For me, the nightmares were the worst.

So when I reflect back on the photo of the statue, I couldn't help but think about the Exorcism Case and the boy involved. The boy was not the question or the key. The question was, "Why did the devil want the family to come here to St. Louis?"

No one has really ever discussed that completely before. I know from my personal experience and from working with these types of cases that there is always a bigger picture, and within that bigger picture is where you will find clarity and truth. The wrong questions have always been asked involving this case. The focus on this case has been completely wrong the whole time. The focus on the boy is really just a rehash of what we already know to be evident. "If it walks like a duck" is the old saying, referring to all things being or behaving in their true nature. There was nothing new or interesting to be found there if you focus on the easy question: "Why the boy?" It *is not* and *should not* be the question at all. You cannot look at just one aspect of a case to find truth and understanding. You need a bigger picture. And sitting in the sun on the porch during that sunny afternoon, this image triggered the question of "Why here?" Then the thoughts began to flow. For a good month afterward, this question and idea captured my imagination, and I went looking for answers. I began to set down the pieces of the puzzle that, in turn, began to fill in the big picture and the truth.

I now know why the devil chose to come here and play. That turns out to be an easy question to answer. He was already here.

Chapter 2
It Begins in Cottage City, Maryland

The year 1949 was the beginning of a period of prosperity for the United States after the war. It was a time when commercialism really began to take hold of the nation. The right appliances, the right food and the right car became the desires of the day. *Death of a Salesman* and *Kiss Me, Kate* were banking on Broadway. "Some Enchanted Evening" and "Diamonds Are a Girl's Best Friend" were songs everyone was listening to. Ten million homes had televisions in them and Americans were watching Ed Sullivan and *The Lone Ranger*. People were going to see *On the Town*, *12 O'clock High*, *All the King's Men*, and *Mighty Joe Young* at the movies. Harry Truman was the current president. People were reading *The Sheltering Sky*, "The Lottery," and George Orwell's *1984*. It was a simpler time and the country was beginning to enjoy itself after the Great Depression and two world wars. This is the world that Roland was living in back in 1949. In order to understand people and comprehend certain situations, one must understand the time period in which they exist. The burgeoning innocence of the late forties is in huge contrast with the evil of the 1949 St. Louis Exorcism. If it was the beginning of the modern age, then the devil was playing in St. Louis to help usher it in fully, completely and diabolically.

I think of a quote from T. S. Elliot's "The Hollow Men" when I think about the possibility of the devil playing and ushering in the modern age, "This is the way the world ends. Not with a bang but a whimper." The demise is slow and without notice. So we sit in our comfortable chairs in our comfortable homes and we do nothing more than slip away into the night without a worry or cause, as long as we know what is on the minds of the Kardashians and the day's top stories we can turn our heads from what is truly happening in our world. This is all without awareness of the effect that evil is having on us in a continual and slow fuck basis. There is a great quote from the *Field Guide to the Apocalypse*, "Don't blame yourself. The apocalypse wasn't your fault. Actually, it was just as much your fault as it was anyone else's. Come to think of it, if you're an American, it was probably about 80–90 percent more your fault than the average human. But don't let that get you down. It wasn't exclusively your fault. Unless you're the president. Then it might be your fault. But you'll have plenty of interns to tell you that it wasn't, so you'll be fine" (Marco).

It could be easily argued that we as a country felt we beat evil to the ground in both of the world wars, and our biggest mistake was not understanding evil would come back stronger and with different means. Capitalism, commercialism, communism, cults, corruption, cash, credit cards, and consumerism are all things that evil can manipulate, and if that is the case, we are all going to be truly guilty in the end. The apocalypse is not going to be broadcast on our cable boxes or computers—well, at least not to a mass audience. How many times have you found yourself surfing the Internet and coming across something you think is nothing more than simple propaganda? You ignore it and you move on. How do you differentiate the truth through the myriad of lies and deceit? It is almost impossible in a world that offers an endless amount of information to distinguish fact from fiction. The actions of diabolical forces would create a smoke screen to hide the truth and leave us wondering. Mark A. Rayner stated brilliantly in *The Fridgularity*, "That's the thing about the collapse of civilization...it never happens according to plan - there's no slavering horde of zombies. No actinic flash of thermonuclear war. No Earth-shuddering asteroid. The end comes in unforeseen ways; the stock market collapses, and then the banks, and then there is no food in the supermarkets, or the communications system goes down completely and inevitably, and previously amiable coworkers find themselves wrestling over the last remaining cookie that someone brought in before all the madness began." He is right, you will never see it coming until you are the one fighting for that last cookie.

Is it such a far-fetched notion to assume that the possession of a teenage boy named Roland could have been a catalyst for the devil to penetrate into society's psyche? How many times have you said to yourself, "It was just a book or it was just a movie"? The truth is, most Americans had never truly considered the idea of the demonic until the movie *The Exorcist*. They lined up for blocks and waited for hours to see what everyone was talking about. The truth was nobody was talking about God. Everyone was talking about the devil. It made the devil himself a superstar. People were fainting in theater lobbies around the world. *The Exorcist* paved the way for *The Omen*, *The Amityville Horror*, *Audrey Rose*, *The Exorcism of Emily Rose*, *The Conjuring,* and many more films that people

31

would flock to the movie theaters to see. This diabolic phenomenon began with one young boy. It's hard not to think that if there is true evil in this world, this was the religious coup of all time and this evil started with Roland.

Innocence and purity are not things you usually combine with the thought of evil. If we accept the idea that evil is able to devour the innocent, that would put us all in danger, wouldn't it? You would prefer that evil goes after what is bad and evil in a person and not what is pure. However, evil hates purity with a passion. This is one of the many tricks that evil plays on mankind. We believe evil would attack those who are diabolically welcoming, but evil people are a waste of time; it is the pure of heart who are the most satisfying and the greatest challenge for diabolical attacks. But is it ever easy to make sense out of the senseless? The idea that a young, innocent boy could have been the victim of one of the most brutal possessions in history seems a hard pill for some of us to swallow.

For the purpose of identification, I will refer to the possessed boy from the 1949 Exorcism Case here as Roland Doe. Although much more is now known about the identity of the boy, I feel the proper reference of identity should be the one given to him by the attending priests. The most accurate telling of the events surrounding Roland Doe's case is the diary of Father Bishop. The diary is effective in recording history, but its job was just that - to act as a device to record events for whatever reason. It was meant to be an internal document and this intent was never meant for public consumption. The problem with Father Bishop's point of view is that he never really asks any questions or presents any theories that detail his perception of the events that took place before, during and after the exorcism. Father Bishop's vague accounts leave too much open to interpretation, and things get lost in the translation of what really went on during those dark days in 1949. There are simply not enough answers to explain why this happened to this young boy. It gives us a framework of facts with no speculation of cause, effect or where the blame should be placed.

After analyzing and dissecting the diary, it's apparent that Roland Doe was victimized by everyone involved. Both Roland's family and the clergy and doctors involved used him for their own gain. Simply analyzing the diary by using "just the facts" is not a logical way to approach such a complex paranormal occurrence. Once you begin to ask the hard questions, the Exorcism Case goes from disturbing to unbelievably horrifying. Roland Doe was a victim of spiritualistic influence, which led to his demise, however, once the diary is dissected, this case becomes much more than just a curious child dabbling in the occult.

The Exorcism Case, along with Father Bishop's diary, began in Cottage City, Maryland. According to *Possessed* by Thomas Allen, Roland Doe's aunt was a spiritualist who introduced Roland to the Ouija board when he expressed a desire to learn how to use it. Some have assumed that Roland invited the demon into his life through the use of the Ouija board. On the surface, this seems to be a plausible assumption. However, as you analyze the diary and take a closer look, this seems to be a very generic reasoning for the boy's demise. There is more here than has actually ever been presented, and the theory behind the Ouija board and the boy's use just doesn't hold up to scrutiny. Was the Ouija board actually the device that was used to invite the demon? To think that Roland reached the state of perfect possession, as defined by the Catholic Church, by using the Ouija board alone does not seem viable or plausible. There is an underlying cause of this boy's possession that has been severely overlooked.

On January 15, 1949, Roland was with his grandmother in her bedroom when they heard a noise that sounded like something dripping. According to the diary, the noise continued until a crucifix shook on the wall as if the wall had been bumped. By the time Roland's parents returned home, there was loud scratching coming from beneath the floorboards near the grandmother's bed. The length of the scratching continued for ten days between the hours of 7:00 p.m. and midnight. The family believed that the scratching was caused by a rodent. After eleven days, the scratching suddenly stopped, so the family thought the rodent died. (Note: this fact was portrayed in Blatty's novel, *The Exorcist*, as well as in the film adaptation.) This type of behavior falls under the infestation stage of possession. However, Roland felt like he was still hearing the noise even though the other family members were not. In possessions, this causes bystanders to begin to question the sanity of the victim experiencing the activity. I would imagine that at this point the boy was also experiencing some type of sleep disturbances, even though it is not stated within the diary. It is also important to note that Roland's spiritualist aunt died on January 26, 1949.

The family did not hear the noise for a period of three days while the boy was still hearing it. After this three-day period, the noise became audible to the entire family once more. It had moved downstairs to the boy's bedroom. The noise had changed to a sound similar to squeaking shoes, and this was only heard at night when the boy went to bed. The sound would move up and down the boy's bed. The squeaking sound continued for six days, and on the sixth night, the scratching became audible again. On this sixth night while lying on the boy's bed, the mother, grandmother, and Roland heard what was described as the rhythm of marching feet and drums.

What happens next raises some interesting questions. The sound traveled back and forth through the mattress. It kept doing so until the mother asked if the sounds were caused by Roland's spiritualist aunt, who had recently passed away. When no response was given, she asked whoever was making the sounds to knock three times. The mother describes this experience as waves of air hitting those on the bed, followed by three knocks on the floor. To clarify that the mother was speaking to the aunt, she asked for the energy to knock four times. Four distinct knocks were heard and then came the sound of clawing on the mattress. When the scratching noises were ignored by the mother and grandmother, the bed would shake violently.

This activity continued until Saturday, February 26, 1949, when scratches appeared on the boy's body over four consecutive nights. Interestingly enough, the scratches appeared in the form of letters on the fourth night. The word "LOUIS" was scratched into the boy's body. The mother took this as an indication that she should bring the boy to St. Louis. Apparently, the mother asked the question in order to find out where she should take her son in order to avoid the home being infested. Following that question, Roland's mother asked the demon when they should leave, and it scratched the word "Saturday" on Roland's body. She then asked how long she should stay in St. Louis, and "3 1/2 Weeks" appeared scratched on his body. The final question she asked was whether she should send the boy to school in St. Louis while they were visiting, and the answer was "no," with the letter *N* appearing on both legs. It is also important to note that all of these scratches caused tremendous pain to the boy.

We have seen this exact type of phenomena reiterated throughout diabolical paranormal cases. The same type of audible haunting noises occurred in the Wateska Wonder Case, the possession of Mary Roff, which happened between 1865 and 1878. Mary Roff was a nineteen-year-old-girl who suddenly became possessed by multiple entities. For several years she had been inflicted with random and unusual fits, which her family thought were the signs of mental instability at first. This was later believed to be the first documented case of possession in America.

Over time, Roland's aunt has been targeted as the catalyst for his possession. However, I'd like to take a moment to present a theory of my own. I feel that the mother had a deeper involvement in Roland's possession than the diary leads us to believe. The mother seemed to have a lot of knowledge about spiritualistic behavior for a God-fearing Lutheran. According to Thomas Allen in *Possessed*, for years the mother had been interested in spiritualism but "would not profess herself as a Spiritualist." In my opinion, this raises some serious questions about the mother's involvement in the case. She was more than just an innocent bystander. It is my inclination that the mother was a practicing spiritualist and was practicing the art of spirit communication with the impressionable young boy. Allen hints that the mother was well versed in spiritualist practices that were taught to her by Roland's aunt.

In the nineteenth and early twentieth century, the Spiritualist Movement was on the rise. Mediumship replaced "the sensitive" as the means of contacting those beyond the grave and communicating with the dead and other spirits. At times, mediums physically allowed a form of possession to take place and the spirits used the mediums as conduits to communicate directly by using the medium's body and voice. Mediums enter into a state of consciousness that is metamorphosed. This state ranges from dissociation to amnesia when trying to recall the events taking place. Even though mediumship involves voluntarily invoking spirits, it sometimes starts off impulsive, and spirits invade a person without being conjured. There is danger involved in practicing spiritualism and mediumship. Religious authorities dispute the true identities of the spirits conjured in spiritualism, emulating that the authentic identities of the possessing spirits are demonic or elemental. Their true intent is to cause deception and possession when called forth.

It is interesting that the spirit possessing Roland answered the mother with words scratched upon the boy's body.

The mother was making a point to clearly communicate with the entity and confirm that it was the dead aunt they were speaking to. It is true the activity was reported to have started two weeks before the aunt's death. But then why was she so sure that it was the dead aunt? The diary alludes to the mother's obsession with communicating with the entity and so does Allen in *Possessed*. The diary also clearly states that the boy was in severe pain every time the scratches would appear on his body. The mother seemed to be more preoccupied with spiritual communication rather than the well-being of the boy. I would even make an accusation that the mother had become morbidly fascinated with the occult and was obsessed with finding the outcome in St. Louis, which I will evidence in a later chapter.

What worries me at this point in the diary is the lack of empathy for Roland Doe by the one person who should have been most empathetic toward him. At a minimum we could assume that the mother was exhibiting signs of Munchausen syndrome by proxy. Munchausen syndrome by proxy, or Factitious Disorder Imposed on Another (FDIA), is an abusive illness and psychiatric disorder where a parent falsifies complaints of bodily symptoms in their children that have no physical or medical basis in order to gain attention or sympathy, even when there is little or nothing tangible for them to gain from the behavior. The mother could have actually enjoyed the attention being bestowed upon her by the horrible things happening to Roland, or it might have been something much deeper and even more diabolic. I believe there might have been a combination of things taking place. The demon preys upon the weakness of the individual, in this case, the mother. A demonic attack is always well conceived and executed. The demon would know that some weakness within the mother craved attention, and the demon possibly knew her deeper desires as well. This is not at all unusual within documented cases of possession. In fact, Mary Roff's parents would often use her as a medium for entertainment during parties and social gatherings at their home. As mentioned in *Child Possessed* by author David St. Clair, a Reverend Dill was helping to host these parties along with the girl's parents at the Roff home, using the young girl's possession to gain attention and admiration from the community. Now the whole idea of Munchausen syndrome by proxy is not too far of a stretch to believe possible in the 1949 Exorcism Case, and this exact behavior has also been demonstrated in similar cases throughout history.

As the descriptions in the diary progress, the escalation of the attack upon Roland increases, but the mother's interests are more focused on the messages she is receiving. Her child is in pain, yet she becomes obsessed with using him to get the answers she thinks she deserves. The boy is not the target at all within this scenario. The target is clearly the mother and the demon is preying on her weaknesses. The love of a mother for her child should be a sacred thing, but for some reason the demon caused a literal disconnect and the mother's love for her son and her concern for him seemingly became superficial.

Because the mother may have dabbled in spiritualism, just as the spiritualist aunt did, it is not a stretch to suggest that she used the aunt's death to her advantage. The mother attempted to take control of the aunt's mental apparatus for her own means. The mental apparatus of someone who has recently passed has lost its guiding power and can be used by evil spirits for any type of use. Because the aunt was a practicing spiritualist, upon death she could be used as a guide to the living. The bargain for this exchange could have led the mother to sell her soul or even sacrifice her son's soul.

Throughout a multitude of spiritual beliefs, including Christianity, the soul of the first-born male is considered to be of utmost importance. Reflect back to the Old Testament scripture where God warns Pharaoh. Pharaoh in return ignores God, only in the end to lose the life of his first-born son. Is it possible that Roland Doe's mother offered up his soul in order to gain more insight into the netherworld? There is evidence within the diary that draws attention to the mother's odd behavior both maternally and religiously.

The diary talks about other manifestations that were taking place during this period of time. An orange and a pear flew across a room when Roland was present. The kitchen table would be upset with any movement on behalf of the boy. Milk and food would be thrown off of the stove. A comb flew "violently" through the air and extinguished blessed candles. In another instance, a Bible was thrown at the feet of the boy without causing him harm.

Other types of activity are discussed in the diary, but the one entry I found interesting is the entry when the Ouija board is mentioned for the first time. It discussed an event that happened to Roland while at school when his desk spun around in a similar fashion to "the plate" on the Ouija board. There is no more explanation than that. Does this mean the Ouija board was still being used for communication at this point? It is not clear and Father Bishop simply makes this entry and then moves on in the diary. The point of the entry was to explain the embarrassment the boy endured and why he no longer went back to school. Of course the demon would choose the easiest way to isolate the boy - by causing humiliation in a very public way and in front of his peers.

The next section of the diary begins to discuss witnesses to the events. There were fourteen different witnesses to the events. However, only a very small portion of these witnesses in Maryland are discussed and none of them to great length. There were two Lutheran ministers who were consulted. One of the ministers asked the boy to spend the night at his home and actually slept with the boy. The clawing sounds were heard that night just like the clawing sounds that were heard at the boy's home. The next statement listed in the diary is quite disturbing. The minster prayed and the activity became stronger and stronger. In retaliation, the minister tied Roland to a chair. There is no explanation as to why this action was either justified or helpful. There is no description of the boy's behavior that constituted such forceful action. Was the boy trying to harm himself or the minister? The diary never reveals. There were other reports about this event where the minister had made a pallet next to his bed and the pallet flew underneath the bed with the boy on it. Roland was levitated over and over beneath the bed, hitting the underneath bed springs and causing cuts to his body. This account came from the minister and not the diary. However, it is also important to note that the Lutheran minister had a fascination with the paranormal, which is evidenced by the letters he was writing back and forth to the Rhine Institute. At this point the boy had to be quite fearful because the people who were entrusted with his well-being seemed to be failing miserably with their irrational and impulsive decisions. We have again seen this throughout historical cases, such as the Mary Roff case.

Meanwhile, the boy becomes more and more isolated. The pain he feels as the words form on his body is excruciating, yet those around him are more concerned with the messages they are receiving. There are some serious questions that should have been raised at this point. Why did the mother instantly assume the ailments and behaviors of her son were caused by paranormal occurrences, more specifically, demonic attack? If these things were happening to your child, any rational parent would think something is physically or psychologically wrong with them. A trip to the psychiatrist should have been the first stop before allowing some inexperienced Lutheran minister to attempt to expel the boy's affliction by tying him to a chair, even if we are to believe the under the bed version told by the minister. Pertaining to possession in the Lutheran faith, " ... one should also not drive out the devil with conjurations," (Mayes) which is exactly what the minister was attempting to do. It was only after the minister's outrageous tactics and inconclusive evaluation that the logical idea of psychological assistance was brought about. Once the boy was taken to the psychiatrist, the psychiatrist makes it clear that he doesn't believe in the paranormal phenomenon taking place. Furthermore, after a multitude of tests, procedures, physicals, and questioning, the psychiatrist determines that the boy is completely normal. His only ailments were a result of his high-strung behavior and irritated demeanor. Irritated seems to be an understatement and under estimation of Roland, considering the multitude of detrimental events he was experiencing at the hands of others.

Another question that raises concerns is why the mother never admitted her involvement in spiritualism. After getting zero answers from the psychiatrist, Roland's family consults none other than a spiritualist. The spiritualist was contacted to rid Roland of the entity that was holding him hostage. But after a lengthy cleansing, the spiritualist had no success. It is revealed here in Father Bishop's diary, however, that the aunt believed very much in spiritualism and often consulted spiritualists. What the diary should have said is, "The family as a whole believed very much in spiritualism and often consulted spiritualists." The mother never openly takes responsibility for opening up her own child to spiritualism, and her child was paying the price for her sins.

Finally, the obvious question comes into play. What is a practicing Lutheran doing asking the Catholic Church for help? Again, according to the Lutheran Pastor-Elder Handbook, " ... one should drive out the devil with and through prayer," and "

... one should drive them out with prayer and contempt. For the devil is a proud spirit, who cannot stand prayer and despising, but desires a ceremony. Therefore, no one should make a ceremony with him, but despise him as much as possible." (Mayes). Not only is the mother not admitting to her spiritualism, but she is also doing exactly what her Lutheran faith forbids her to do, which is seek out a *ceremony* with the devil. In this reference, it's an exorcism.

For the first time in the diary, mention of the parent's consultation with a Catholic priest appears. After hearing the family's experiences concerning Roland, the priest recommends blessed candles, holy water and definite prayers. The diary clearly states the priest did not meet Roland in person at this time. This is an extremely abnormal response to those seeking spiritual guidance from a priest for another, especially one who is a child. The priest should have insisted to see the boy in order for him to make an evaluation and, at a minimum, attempt to perform a blessing on him. You never know—at this stage, a simple blessing may have been all that was needed to suppress the attack from within. No one will ever know because the priest did not bother to see the boy in person, if we are to believe the descriptions in the diary.

After evaluating this part of the diary, it occurred to me that we are clearly seeing the effects of diabolical oppression play out with every person the boy had come in contact with. Those people were supposed to protect Roland, but his mother, grandmother, father, minister, doctor, psychiatrist, spiritualist, teacher, and his priest all failed him. The demon working on Roland's soul had penetrated the conscious of his most beloved and trusted mentors, influencing them to slowly isolate Roland one by one. Since the priest did not offer to bless the home, the mother gathered up the holy materials and tried to purge her home of negative energy. According to the diary, the mother took the holy water and sprinkled it all through the rooms of the house, even though this went against her faith as a Lutheran.

When she placed the bottle of holy water upon the shelf, it flew off onto the floor; however, it did not break. When the mother lit the blessed candle and placed it next to Roland's bed, the activity increased and the mattress that Roland and his mother were laying on began to sway back and forth. Of course this was the end result because the mother was again defying her own faith for that of another doctrine. Martin Luther himself states, " ... and if anyone wants to drive them out as was done at that time [of the Apostles], he tempts God" (Mayes). This means as a Lutheran, the use of holy water, blessed candles, and such are nothing more than a ceremony for the devil, which in turn tempts God - which is sin.

At this point in the diary, Father Bishop makes a statement insinuating that he was perplexed by the lack of involvement from the Maryland priest, as well as his negligence and impropriety. After the mother reported the events that took place while blessing the home to the Maryland priest, it was all hands on deck for the priest. Realizing that the mother's attempt at blessing the home had aggravated the entity, he pursued permission from the bishop of the Catholic Church to perform an exorcism on the boy. In Catholicism, a formal exorcism is only legitimate with the permission of the bishop. The Rite of Exorcism is led by a priest or bishop who is commonly referred to as an exorcist. The exorcism itself consists of a series of prayers, blessings, and commands guided by the exorcist, who attempts to drive out evil spirits in cases of demonic possession. The Maryland priest's attempt to obtain permission for an exorcism is a clear indication that the priest acknowledges his error in judgment. According to the Lutheran Pastor-Elder Handbook, all things happen by prayers and if the desired effect is not immediately followed remember the decisions of exorcists are not always effective. I think the important thing to keep in mind here is neither the Lutheran nor the Catholic faith in themselves are evil, but going against a communed faith is evil and that plays into the devil's hands. If you are a Lutheran, it is not wise to seek the council of a spiritualist or a priest to deal with the devil. To do so goes against personal faith, which is a win-win situation for the devil.

It is not stated in the diary if the Maryland priest met with the boy face-to-face. However, one would assume that he had to have collected enough proof from Roland Doe in order to pursue permission from the bishop. Before the Maryland priest could commence the exorcism process, the family was already on their way to St. Louis, Missouri. There is a later report from another source that claims the priest did indeed perform a failed attempt at exorcism before the boy left for St. Louis. We will cover this pre-St. Louis exorcism claim later in the book when it becomes more relevant to the story.

When looking at the early activity in Father Bishop's diary, it amazes me the speed at which the case progressed through the stages of possession. I am also astonished by the magnitude of mistakes that were made by the adults involved. Even though the diary does not directly state when and how the invitation occurred with Roland, it is undeniable how rapid the activity accelerated from the infestation to the oppression stage. The question now remains, why did a strict Lutheran family embrace the rites of spiritualism and Catholicism time and time again if there was no underlying motive? It seems to be out of the ordinary for a Lutheran mother to jump at the opportunity to openly communicate with an entity that was holding her son's body hostage. Her quick attempt to contact the dead aunt gives way to suspicion. She seemingly expected, suspected, or knew that something about the aunt's death was the catalyst for her son's possession. There was less motherly compassion and empathy for her son's well-being and more emphasis on the answers received by the spirit afflicting Roland.

 With the rise of interest in paranormal investigations and the endless search for the "most haunted" locations, there has been a lot of recent attention and fascination placed on the house in the suburbs of St. Louis where Roland spent a series of days. However, the attention on this location may be misplaced. Most priests and exorcists would tell you that in any demonic case, the doorway that allowed the demon to enter should be the focal point. I also think it is interesting how the film, inspired by William Peter Blatty's novel, is still, after all these years, dictating society's reaction and perception of the 1949 Exorcism Case. In some way it could allude to the fact that the film itself acts like a smoke screen to keep the public eye away from the authentic locations, which are the true epicenters of the case. After analyzing Father Bishop's diary and dissecting research related to the case, the truth to how the case was handled by the family, the Church, and society will come to light and new theories will open your eyes to the hidden intendment.

Chapter 3
The Ouija Board

The Ouija board has always been shrouded in mystery and skepticism. According to historians and popular cultural experts, the board's origins are a complete mystery. There has been continued controversy surrounding the board as a tool to communicate with the dead. It is evident the board's popularity in the United States was fueled by the hard-hitting Spiritualism Movement. In an article about the history of the Ouija board for *Smithsonian.com*, McRobbie writes that "Spiritualism worked for Americans: it was compatible with Christian dogma, meaning one could hold a séance on Saturday night and have no qualms about going to church the next day. It was an acceptable, even wholesome activity to contact spirits at séances, through automatic writing, or table turning parties, in which participants would place their hands on a small table and watch it begin shake and rattle, while they all declared that they weren't moving it" (2013). This is important to point out when we look at Roland Doe's mother and the strange dichotomy between her beliefs as a Christian woman and the obvious knowledge of spiritualism that she demonstrates throughout the case. However, the question remains, was there something more sinister taking place below the surface? In order to further examine the mother's role within the possession, we need to take a hard look at spiritualism and its connection with the Ouija board.

In 1886, the Ouija board made its appearance in the Associated Press, offering an innovative way to conjure spirits in a spiritualist camp in Ohio. Advertisements for the ominous talking board began to appear in the United States in February 1891 from the Kennard Novelty Company (McRobbie). The board appeared at this time in the exact same way we are familiar with it today. The board was not revered as something possibly evil at that time but was accepted and promoted without question. I think it is important to note that is was pure greed that drove the mysterious board into the living rooms of America. The Ouija board was viewed as a game and the consequences of using such a tool were overlooked. It was sold by a toy company and they viewed the board as nothing more than a moneymaker that would cater to the growing American interest in spiritualism. Ironically enough, William Fuld, who was running the company by 1927, took a deadly fall from the roof of his new factory. It was the Ouija board that told him to build it.

There have been numerous theories throughout the years to suggest how the board works, but these theories are just that. However, for the sake of the board's connection to the Spiritualism Movement, it is important to look at famed occultist and spiritualist Aleister Crowley, who called himself the Beast. Interestingly enough, Crowley was among the first to warn about the misuse of the board and its dangers. In *Aleister Crowley and the Ouija Board*, author J. Edward Cornelius points out that Crowley warned that certain elementals "have the ability to communicate through the board and can take on the guise of whomever *we* want them to be. Since these entities have the ability to exist by mutation within the lunar or astral light, they are also known as shape-shifters." These entities are the easiest to summon through the board and can take the energy to get access into our world. Crowley believes it was not the board itself that was the doorway to spirit; it was the planchette.

A great development in spirit automatic writing was achieved by French spiritualist M. Planchette in 1853 with the invention of the planchette. Automatic writing is the spirit using the hand of the medium to write scribbles on a piece of paper. The planchette made communication easier to achieve. The planchette is a wooden, heart shaped or triangular device with two wooden legs and a pencil on the tip of the triangle. The legs of the planchette are on tiny casters, which make it easier for it to move around on the paper. But how exactly does the planchette work? According to Cornelius, the triangle acts as a "between state," neither part of this world nor the spiritual world. It is a doorway that swings both ways between worlds. The power of the triangle is seen throughout history and in every magickal grimoire. It is within the triangle that a magician will summon a discarnate entity in order to communicate with them, bind them and control them. Simply stated, the use of the triangle to communicate with spirits has been around for centuries. The danger is in the misuse in effecting a gateway into the invisible world without the knowledge and ability to control what is being summoned. The danger is not and never has been with the board or the planchette itself. The danger lies within the inability of a person using these items to control what they are communicating with. I have said this same exact thing for years now.

Plain and simple, if you are going to use the board, do not use it as a toy and do not use it unless you are capable of dealing with what you are communicating with. It is important to realize that a true spiritualist is not, on a personal note, trying to contact spirits or even famous people who have passed. The true spiritualist will try to connect with an elemental or, in this reference, a demon. Crowley explains, "To invoke is to call in just as to evoke is to call forth. It is very easy for these elementals to become anything they want you to believe they are. They can make you believe that they are anyone you want to speak with. They are tricksters and can be very dangerous" (1976). Who they become depends completely on the type of questions you ask internally and externally. They can read your mind. They know what you are thinking. They will be ten steps ahead of you because they know more about you than you know about yourself.

When Roland Doe's mother shows interest in communicating with the entity afflicting her son, it tells us a lot about the case. The mother may have been communicating with the dead aunt previous to Roland's possession. But was she really communicating with the aunt, or something more sinister? I believe in the latter. The mother was so obsessed with communicating with the dead aunt that she failed to realize that this behavior was a danger to Roland. At this point, she believed the elemental or demon she was interacting with and she would stop at nothing to find answers. The boy was nothing more than a conduit for this communication because he was offered up by the mother for the elemental's use. Whatever the case, what this moment tells us immediately is that the boy was not the only one in communication. The mother was just as guilty of this communication, if not even more responsible, because she was the adult who was responsible for the spiritual and physical well-being of her son. It becomes too complicated at this point to believe the boy would have ever been completely responsible on his own, and the diary is the source giving us this insight. The truths are hiding within the facts of this case. Personally, I find it terrifying that Roland Doe's mother could have been his afflicter. Her reckless behavior and emotionless reactions for Roland Doe's condition are frightening.

I find it amusing when I see certain paranormal shows try to contact the demon by using a board or to try to exorcise the house in St. Louis. It was not the point of origination. The true oracle that acts as a passageway to the netherworld is the planchette. So unless the investigators have the original planchette used by Roland Doe, their attempts and efforts are fruitless. I also believe the planchette was not only used by Roland but his mother as well. The mother was the facilitator in this whole case, whether willingly or not. Sometimes people lose their way in their faith, unable to find their way back. Her spiritual journey was spiraling out of control. She was using her son to make a connection with elementals or demons. The original planchette, used in the epicenter location (Cottage City, Maryland) is the gateway to Roland's demon. I am hoping and praying that this planchette was destroyed or lost years ago - that it never gets into the wrong hands. If it still exists, it is a dangerous device with a tremendous amount of negativity surrounding it. The physical locations are actually inconsequential to this case. They only hold remnants of the negative energy. The true holy grail of this case would be the ultimate point or origination: the planchette.

Now here is the most frightening part of this theory. Crowley explains that a demon or elemental will feed upon children because they are so open and vulnerable (1976). They emit endless energy that the demon or elemental will feed on. Whether the mother meant it or not, Roland was the food and power supply for the demon. Once the possession came into play, he became the oracle for the mother's questions, and she no longer needed the planchette. The elemental or demon was using the boy as a vessel and the most horrific aspect is that his mother found out and allowed it to continue. By the time this is mentioned in Father Bishop's diary, it is apparent she had been carrying on with this behavior for some time. As the demon became stronger, it was easy for her to communicate with it. Her actions prove the escalation of the possession of Roland were her fault. He was her oracle. He was her communication piece. At this point, we could label her behavior as spiritual neglect for her child. Roland's mother was a spiritual "Mommie Dearest," if you will. At what point does she wake up and realize the damage she is doing to her child? Is she so far spiritually and faithfully misguided that even the suffering of her child cannot bring her back? Perhaps it was after she dabbled in spiritualism when she realized she was in over her head. Or perhaps it was after the boy was transported to St. Louis.

Chapter 4
Welcome to St. Louis

Roland Doe arrived with his family to the suburbs of St. Louis, Missouri, in early March of 1949. In reference to Father Bishop's diary, the events that took place in St. Louis were listed day by day with full descriptions. The first dated entry, on March 7, 1949, describes a séance that was arranged by Roland's family. It took place at the residence of Roland's aunt and uncle. It is stated that five to six other relatives were present. Also in attendance was what is described as an "alphabet medium" to contact the spirit afflicting Roland. The family is once again turning to a spiritualist to contact the entity to ask it questions. The medium used some form of automatic writing that uses a configuration of the alphabet. The boy was the oracle, the human planchette, in which the séance was circled around.

The automatic writing session was carried out on a porcelain sink table in the kitchen. Letters were written on a piece of paper, and individual letters were underlined as the table would move. They began to receive messages. They were told that the spirit was not the devil but the spirit of the deceased aunt. The diary also described the responses from the entity in regards to its identity.

The spirit was asked to confirm that it was in fact the deceased aunt. It moved a heavy bed two or three feet in response. There were no bystanders near the bed. All family members that were present witnessed this occurrence. Once again writing appeared on Roland's body with a sharp pain. There are no specifics as to what was written on his body. However, an earlier report in the diary alluded to an event when the words "NO SCHOOL" appeared on his body. This was in St. Louis, so what these two entries tell us is that once again the boy's pain is being disregarded, and the questioning is continuing. Then Roland goes to bed and is unable to sleep that night because of the shaking of the bed and the clawing sounds on the mattress. Not only is the boy going through actual hell on earth, but there are times stated in the diary when the shaking of the mattress starts and family members get into bed with the boy to experience it for themselves. It almost seems as if the boy was some type of circus show oddity to this family of obvious spiritualists, who are amazed and titillated by the events that were occurring.

Tuesday, March 8, 1949-

In the very next entry there were more descriptions of the mattress shaking and the return of the clawing sounds. During this incident, a cousin was sleeping with Roland. The diary elaborated by saying, "[The] mattress continued to move in the direction of the uprights of the bed, even when cousins lay alongside of R." Sleep deprivation is a very serious thing, and a demon will often use sleep deprivation to weaken the person it is trying to possess. Lack of sleep weakens the resolve, will and strength of a person. One can only imagine the physical deterioration of this human being. Another question has to be why the family would risk exposing other children to this madness -

58

the cousins were also in danger at this point. Remember what Crowley tells us about the openness of a child's spirit and the attraction to the youth's energy source. Because these events were so horrific, children should have been the last to be in attendance. Yet time and time again this family risks exposing these children for whatever reason. Interestingly enough, it was one of Roland's Catholic cousins who finally made the smartest move out of the entire family. Upon witnessing Roland's behavior, the cousin asks Father Bishop, one of the clerical professors at St. Louis University, for assistance. Finally, someone makes the proper step to see there is something horrific going on here and realizes the boy needs assistance from the Church and not the assistance of every medium and crackpot in a three-hundred-mile radius. Father Bishop consults with other priests, one being the president of St. Louis University, and they decide that a blessing will help the boy, agreeing to have Father Bishop administer it.

Finally, someone steps forward to help Roland. I have to say it amazes me that out of all of these adults, it was a younger person who took the correct steps to find help. But it is important to remember: the mother brought the boy to St. Louis not because they were there to seek help, but because the entity told her to. It seems obvious that she came to St. Louis out of curiosity and not because she was pursuing religious guidance. Along with the family, she continued to use every avenue possible to continue communication with the entity haunting her child.

In relation to the family's bizarre actions in St. Louis, this would be a good place to discuss the supposed failed exorcism by the priest in Maryland, which was mentioned earlier. There are reports out there that mention an unsuccessful exorcism that was attempted in Maryland before bringing the boy to St. Louis. The diary never mentions this unsuccessful exorcism. Remember, the diary talks about the priest trying to get permission for an exorcism, but he is unsuccessful because the boy is moved to St. Louis. However, I have heard that some priests claimed that he actually performed an exorcism on the boy without the bishop's permission. The claims suggest it ended with Roland managing to loosen a bedspring that he used to make a long cut on the priests forearm. There are other reports that state this exorcism was performed with the permission of the Jesuits and was attempted at Georgetown University Hospital.

According to *Possessed* by Allen, "Roland was referred to a Roman Catholic priest, the Rev. Edward Hughes. Hughes reported giving a bottle of holy water and candles to Roland's parents to give to Roland before he went to sleep. The parents said the telephone table on which the holy water sat smashed into hundreds of pieces while the candle flamed up, torching the ceiling. Hughes then had his request granted to have an exorcism performed. The attempt was made at Georgetown University Hospital, but it failed."

There are different possible scenarios here. Father Bishop could have been trying to protect the renegade Maryland priest in the diary by not mentioning the failed exorcism. The other possibility is that Father Bishop did not know about the failed exorcism. However, there is another account where a female cousin of Roland tells Father Bishop about the failed Maryland exorcism when she approaches him for guidance for her possessed cousin. There is another way to dissect Father Bishop's actions, which later lead to urban legend. I am not sure why Father Bishop would avoid speaking about the failed exorcism because it would be a critical part of this case. Also, we need to keep in mind Father Bishop's diary was written to record the history of the case for the Church and was not necessarily meant for public consumption. Smoke screens were being raised, but why? What secrets was the Church trying to hide? One thing is without question, the diary raises a lot of queries about the truth surrounding the case and especially the sympathy toward Roland's parents. The diary clearly paints a whole different picture of them, in particular his mother.

Chapter 5
Father Bishop's Blessing

What is a blessing? Seems like a simple question with a simple answer at first. Father William P. Saunders describes a blessing as follows, "Blessings come under the category of sacramentals. A sacramental is a special prayer, action or object that, through the prayers of the Church, prepares a person to receive grace and to better cooperate with it. One example is when we make the sign of the cross using holy water when entering a church. That pious action and the holy water itself, which together remind us of our baptism, awaken us to the presence of God and dispose us to receiving God's grace." For those who are suffering under oppression (or if it has progressed to possession) then the blessing prepares the person to receive the grace and better cooperate with it. The blessing takes ordinary objects from the world and gives them a holy purpose. These objects become powerful items with extreme positive energy and God's grace. The power within these objects becomes an effective and powerful tool to repel pure evil. Holy water would be considered one of these items, along with blessed salts, oils, crucifixes, candles, and relics of the saints.

I have had the unique and rare opportunity to have had an extreme oppression lifted from myself during my personal demonic haunting. I was fortunate the blessing clutched on so quickly and I did not need an abundance of blessings, or even worse, a full-blown exorcism. As I reflect, I can remember the father asking me to close my eyes as he laid his hand upon the top of my head. As soon as he began to pray, I could feel the evil lurking within. Interestingly enough, Catholicism is not my faith, and in fact, at the time I was struggling with my faith in general. So one could imagine how shocked I was by the physical reaction my body was having to Catholic blessings, as the father began to pray. I could not breathe, almost like a severe asthma attack. I was sweating profusely even though it was a cool autumn day. I was on the brink of passing out, breathing quick shallow breaths, and it felt as if I had an elephant sitting on my chest. But through all this chaos, I could still hear the priest praying, fighting for my soul. Just when I thought I could not stand it anymore and I wanted to give up, I saw three bright white flashes, which made an audible sound in my ears. As each flash ascended forth, air found its way back into my lungs and I felt this overwhelming sense of peace and calm. It was a feeling of euphoria and I wanted it to remain with me forever. I felt so clean from within. It was that grace Father Saunders spoke of in the introductory passage.

Wednesday, March 9, 1949-

The first blessing was to be administered by Father Bishop in the suburban house in St. Louis. Father Bishop blessed the entire house while bestowing a special blessing upon Roland and his bed. Father Bishop pinned a second-class relic of St. Margaret Mary to the far corner of Roland's pillow using a safety pin. As soon as Roland went to bed,

64

the mattress began to shake toward the uprights of the bed. Roland lay perfectly still and, as stated in Bishop's diary, "he did not exert any physical effort." The movement finally subsided after fifteen minutes, ceasing completely when Father Bishop made a sign of the cross with Saint Ignatius holy water on the bed. The movement began once again when the father stepped out of the room for a moment. During the fifteen minutes of movement, Roland cried out in extreme pain. The mother immediately raised the boy's clothes to reveal "zigzag scratches" on the boy's abdomen in bold red lines. We can only guess she was looking for some type of answer or message somewhere on the child. The boy had been under the watchful eyes of six other people during the whole fifteen minutes, so he could not have done it to himself. When the mattress finally subsided that night, there were no further disturbances. The time was noted at 11:15 p.m.

At this point, it appears that the boy was in an acute stage of diabolical oppression. The paranormal activity that surrounded the boy served several purposes, especially those weakening his will. The most apparent aspect of his behavior was his inability to move during these series of events, his world unraveling before and around him. What we do not know is his mental state at this point. What was he thinking? He seems to be settling into the exhaustion. Only when he endures the extreme pain of the scratches does he cry out. The instant the scratches appear, he is humiliated with showing his body to a room full of people searching for answers. Keep in mind: this is a fourteen-year-old boy who is in the middle of puberty and all that it entails. It is another form of the demonic attack. Sometimes, when a doorway to the demonic is opened through the occult within a family, it is like a huge welcome sign for generations to come.

Thursday, March 10, 1949-

The shaking of the boy's bed starts again; however, this time the scratching sounds create a beat that sounds like marching soldiers. The second-class relic of St. Margaret Mary is mysteriously unpinned and thrown to the floor. Roland jumps with a fright when the relic is thrown. The word "fright" is used in the diary to describe Roland and his emotions during the possession. For the first time, this could be an indication that the boy has realized the danger he is in. The throwing of the relic is a clear sign of demonic revulsion toward anything associated with God. It is demonstrating its hate, and with the boy's reaction, I would think it is removing the relic in order to do further damage.

This is the second time in the diary that there is a mention of marching sounds, hinting at "an arriving army." Mark 5:9 from the Bible reads of Jesus questioning a possessed man, "And Jesus asked him, 'What is your name?' He replied, 'My name is Legion, for we are many.'" The interesting factor is that the diabolic retaliated to Father Bishop's blessing by sending an army to battle over Roland's soul. Once the army increased in mass, the demon soldiers removed the relic of protection with their added ranks. The "diabolical army" was preparing for battle. Spiritual warfare literally is "warfare." The diabolic army was making their stand for battle. It is not uncommon for the sound of marching soldiers to accompany a demonic event. When this happens, it usually proves the fight for the soul of the possessed is going to be very long and difficult.

It is clear to me that during the events of the blessing, Father Bishop realized the need for further assistance. Deep in his mind, Father Bishop was planning his own army for battle by calling on angels during his blessing. It really is as literal as that when we are dealing with things of this nature. The New Testament mentions Satan thirty-six times in thirty-three verses, and the book of Revelation tells of "that ancient serpent, who is called the devil and Satan, the deceiver of the whole world," being thrown down to the earth together with his angels. In Luke 10:18, Jesus says: "I saw Satan fall like lightning from heaven." The angels who fell with Satan are the legion, and it is clear they were readying for the onslaught of the battle to come.

Chapter 6
The Arrival of Spiritual Reinforcement

There are some priests who, when they read this Gospel passage, this and others, say: 'But, Jesus healed a person with a mental illness.' They do not read this, no? It is true that at that time, they could confuse epilepsy with demonic possession; but it is also true that there was the devil! And we do not have the right to simplify the matter, as if to say: 'All of these (people) were not possessed; they were mentally ill.' No! The presence of the devil is on the first page of the Bible, and the Bible ends as well with the presence of the devil, with the victory of God over the devil.
- Pope Francis, Oct. 11, 2013

When does one make the decision to put themselves in the line of fire? What keeps a man like Father Bishop from running the other way in the face of true evil? Surely he must have had deep knowledge that he was endangering his soul. It would have been easy to turn his back and walk the other way, but he stayed to help the boy. Did he know the full history of the boy and his family? Those who knew Roland eluded that he was a cruel and troubled child, an outcast among his peers. Did Father Bishop hear the rumors about a child who some say killed animals for fun? Was he aware of the mother's obsession with the ideals of the Spiritualist Movement? Or even worse, did Father Bishop believe there were deeper issues - that Roland may have been sexually abused as other priests have suggested throughout the years? Perhaps all of this is just urban legend: theories that have been kicked around for years. By all accounts, everything we have heard or come to know about the boy has been hearsay. The majority of eyewitness testimony referred to the boy like any other boy his age, even at times a sweet child. Research over the years has suggested that Roland, now an old man, cannot remember anything from his ordeal. It could easily be argued that the boy could have been showing signs of attachment for a long time before the actual possession. It could be argued that it wasn't something that started almost overnight. It was something that took its time and weaved a very complicated web of deception. Was Father Bishop aware that he was standing at the epicenter of a perfect diabolical storm? With all of these questions going through his mind, Father Bishop knew something that lead him to believe he could not handle Roland on his own, that he needed help. The diary does very little to answer these questions. However, the entry for Friday, March 11, 1949, gives us a small glimpse of Father Bishop's thoughts through his actions.

Friday, March 11, 1949-

At the beginning of the diary entry, it becomes clear Father Bishop felt he could not handle this case on his own. It is on that date that we are introduced to the involvement of Father Bowdern, who was the pastor of St. Francis Xavier College Church on the campus of St. Louis University. In honor of St. Francis Xavier, Father Bowdern felt it would be a good idea to bring the corresponding relic for a Novena blessing; he also carried with him first-class relics of North American martyrs and the saint Peter Canisius. He was obviously arming himself for a battle, which shows Father Bishop and Father Bowdern were both very concerned.

The boy went to bed around 11:00 p.m. that night. Shortly after going to bed, the boy called downstairs that he was afraid because a "strong force" had thrown an object at the mirror in the bedroom. It turned out the object was none other than the opened pin of St. Margaret Mary. The diary explains that it sounded like a "pallet striking the glass." There was also a scratch mark in the shape of a cross on Roland's outer forearm. The pain was described like being scratched by a thorn. The cross remained on the boy's arm for approximately forty-five minutes, and then it was completely gone. Father Bowdern read the Novena of Grace prayer to St. Francis Xavier. He blessed Roland with a relic, which contained a bone fragment from St. Francis Xavier's forearm. Then, what is described as a crucifix relic was pinned underneath the boy's pillow. At this point, there was no scratching or shaking of the mattress. After the blessing, the group of observers went back downstairs to go over details of the case history. There was a sudden loud crash that came from Roland's room. A bottle of Saint Ignatius holy water was thrown two feet outside the boy's room. The bookcase next to the bed was turned to face the entrance to the room. The stool from the dressing table traveled two feet to the bed. The family moved the stool back to where it belonged and within two minutes it was flipped completely over. The St. Mary Margaret relic was "lost in the room." Violent shaking of the bed began and rhythmic scratching followed.

The next entry in the diary is not only infuriating, but it also answers the family's true involvement with the demon. It eludes that the family desperately continues to contact and communicate with the entity, even through it seemed to escalate the activity with Roland. The diary states, "The five people in the room decided to ask questions of the spirit. The family asked about a hidden fortune which belonged to the deceased spiritualist aunt. They questioned the demon about the money's whereabouts and received the message that they would find a map stored in a strong box in an attic." We now have a motive for the mother's action. Money was the motivating force for this family's line of questioning and why the boy was being used as a vessel or oracle. He was the human planchette to find where the aunt hid the money.

At this moment, it is important to discuss greed in its reference to the diabolical. Throughout the years I have seen many priests refuse payment for helping with demonic cases. I have even known of priests who have torn up checks in front of clients. Why? The answer is simple: if allowed, the demon will use and dilute the work of the faithful with greed. When monetary funding enters into a case, it becomes a catalyst for destruction. The demon will use this greed to attack its victims and weaken those trying help. In paranormal investigation, prospective clients are advised to take caution. Greed is one of the seven deadly sins. It often leads to temptation and the spell of other sins. The connection to the Faustian legend here is undeniable. In his 1999 article for the *New York Times*, Albert Manguel discusses the legend of Dr. Faust and its implications throughout history,
At wine-and-cheese parties and on afternoon talk shows, we like to say that history repeats itself and that historical characters return in new disguises. We speak of Milosevic as a new Hitler, Neil Armstrong as a new Columbus. Such associations rarely work, because facts get in the way of these

comfortable equations. More interesting (for me), less insidious, more revealing, is to muse on fictional characters who have become real in our collective imagination, and try to see where their endless transformations have led them, here and in our time. What has become of Job, of Huckleberry Finn, of Lady Macbeth? And my favorite, Doctor Faust?

Within the realm of fiction we see characters who, although fictionalized, are based on the human experience. The story of Dr. Faust is a morality tale. In the story, Faust sold his soul to the devil because of his greed. His bargain with the devil required his renouncement of his Christian faith. In return, for twenty-four years, the devil agreed to answer all of Faust's questions and grant all of his wishes. In the end, the devil tears Faust's body apart and claims possession of his soul. Manguel elaborates, "In all probability, this legendary Faust was based on two historical figures: one Georg Sabellicus who, in the first years of the sixteenth century, boasted of performing all the miracles of Christ; and a certain Johann Faust of Simmern who, in 1532, was denied entry into Nuremberg for being known as a 'great sodomite and necromancer.'"

Morality tales often find their way into real-life circumstances. In the 1949 Exorcism Case, the relationship between Roland and his mother plays out similar to the Faust legend. On December 22, 2014, Pope Francis warns about the sickness of greed in a speech from the Vatican, "It is the sickness of the rich fool who thinks he will live for all eternity, and of those who transform themselves into masters and believe themselves superior to others, rather than at their service" (Zaimov). Clearly this mother should have been at the service of her child. But instead of doing what a mother should do, she in turn not only sold her soul to the devil, but potentially sold the soul of her child. Roland's mother did not weigh the consequences, much like Dr. Faust. Blinded by the pursuit of this mysterious fortune, she completely forgets her responsibility as a mother who's supposed to care for her son's spiritual health.

Many characteristics found within the fictional Dr. Faust can be seen in Roland's mother. Historical events and morality tales go hand in hand and can be clearly outlined in every religion known to man. The Bible warns in 1 Timothy 6:9, "But those who desire to be rich fall into temptation, into a snare, into many senseless and harmful desires that plunge people into ruin and destruction." Buddha warns, "Inflamed by greed, incensed by hate, confused by delusion, overcome by them, obsessed in mind, a man chooses for his own affliction, for others' affliction, for the affliction of both, and experiences pain and grief " (Carrithers).

Greed was the diabolical invitation to summon the demon. Anytime we allow ourselves to be driven by greed, we are allowing the diabolical to enter and to be close to our souls. We can see an example of this in Roland's Lutheran mother when she turned to occultism to satisfy her greed. It is the same thing Faust did in the legend. Her lack of willpower is mind-boggling. The fact that Roland's family turned their backs on their faith so quickly explains why the attack was so abrupt and violent. In reference to the diary entries that speak of the family's struggle with faith, a theory has arisen. My theory about the use of the Ouija board in relation to the family's demise rings true. In pursuit of the spiritualist aunt's money, the Ouija board opened the door to a path of greed. I am sure that if this were the case, they would be given clues to keep them asking more and more questions. As this questioning continued, the attachment would have started to take hold. Because of the boy's closeness with the aunt, I am sure the mother thought he would be able to get the answers they were seeking. They might have even let the boy use the board by himself in hopes of getting answers. He may have been encouraged to use the board by himself for that purpose.

The signs of diabolical infestation began with the scratching noises, and the boy may have been coaxed in communicating with the entity without knowing the harmful repercussions. Even though danger ensued, the family must have made progress in their pursuit of the money because they kept encouraging the boy to use the Ouija board. Because the diary lacks detail about Roland's father's involvement, he might have been skeptical and disengaged, and that could be why we do not hear too much about him at this point. He might have been looking for logical explanations pertaining to the scratching. He may have thought it was a rodent of some sort, which was stated in the diary. However, I think the mother felt she was getting closer to answers and knew this activity was spiritual, so she continued the process of questioning. Reflecting back on the night when the mother was on the bed and asked the entity if it was that of the aunt, it became clear the mother's intentions were deceptive. By this time, she had already realized the power of her son's abilities and knew he was the communication vessel - a living planchette. She transported the boy to St. Louis not looking for help, but following the clue she was given from the scratches on Roland's chest. Her main motivation to travel to St. Louis was the dead aunt's hidden fortune. My theory at this point in the case is evident. The boy is not only a demonic victim, but the victim of his own mother's greed.

Chapter 7
Permission Granted

We turn to the Church at times when we
are in need. We hope to find that angel on earth who
will help to deliver us from the grips of evil.
Gaining that help is not always an easy task. It is
always in those final moments when you feel that
all help is lost and can never be attained when help
arrives. I have seen numerous cases through the
years where it has been necessary to fight to gain
the help that is being so desperately sought, and that
includes my own situation. The truth is, we all are
the masters of our own lives, and it is essential we
understand how we participate in our own
hauntings. A haunting is not always something that
should be considered paranormal. We can be
haunted by many different things, such as grief,
phobias, or horrific memories. I have seen many
different types of haunted people throughout the
years, and when I look at Roland, I see a boy who
was not only paranormally haunted but also
emotionally haunted. He was haunted paranormally
and he was haunted by the reaction of those around
him and the victimization by those who were
supposed to protect him.

The simple faith that a child puts into those
around them should never be something that needs

to be earned. It should have been unconditional. Under the circumstances, it would be a further injustice to view him as someone who was faking it. It is easier to grasp onto his unusual behavior in order to justify, rationalize, or understand what happened to this fourteen-year-old boy. The fact remains he was just that, a boy - a boy who may have been screaming out for help long before anyone might have understood or even realized he was in trouble, whether you want to consider it paranormal or psychological.

It is hard to imagine the pain and the fear he must have been experiencing in the confines of that bedroom as his world was quickly spinning out of control. He may have felt defective in some way. Being an only child, his relationship with his dead aunt must have been very sacred to him. He was probably confused as to why someone he loved so deeply would be hurting him. He lay there in pain while the parents and priests were standing around him alluding to the fact that the aunt was causing the pain and scratches he endured. In Roland's mind, this was probably quite confusing because his aunt was someone he admired, revered, and cherished.

Wednesday, March 16, 1949-

Permission was granted by the Most Reverend Archbishop Joseph E. Ritter for an exorcism. Father Bowdern was the one who was allowed to read the prayers of exorcism, according to the Roman Ritual. The scene was set for one of the most iconic moments in the history of true horror. Between 10:15 and 10:30 p.m., Father Bowdern, Father Bishop, and Mr. W. Halloran S.J., who would later become a priest, arrived at the home. Who can forget that iconic moment from *The Exorcist* when the exorcist, Father Marin, steps from the cab in front of the foggy house as the demon screamed from inside? I imagine this was what the scene was like on that March evening in 1949. No one in that quiet neighborhood had a clue about the battle of good and evil that was about to take place in the quaint brick house on that quiet suburban street in Missouri.

Shortly after 10:30 p.m., Roland was sent to bed and Father Bowdern helped the boy make an act of contrition. After this, everyone was called into the room to prepare for the exorcism. Father Bishop, Halloran, and Roland's mother, aunt, and uncle were present in the room. Everyone knelt beside Roland's bed and they said prayers together. Roland recited the prayers with them. Next, robed in surplice and stole, Father Bowdern began the prayers of exorcism, beginning with Praecipio, or the direct instructions. Upon the first Praecipio, "three large parallel bars" were scratched upon the boy's stomach. As Father Bowdern continued, scratches appeared on the boy's legs, thighs, stomach, back, chest, face and throat. The scratches were very painful and were raised up almost like thin lacerations, which bled slightly. Roland said that some of the scratches felt like thorns, while others felt like brands. The brands he stated were the most painful. Appearing on Roland's right leg was a picture of the devil, and the word "HELL" appeared on his chest. These reappeared during the second Praecipio when Father Bowdern demanded the demon identify itself. According to the diary, "The devil was portrayed in red. His arms were held above his head and seemed to be webbed, giving the hideous appearance of a bat." There were several responses that were given from the entity throughout prayer. One was the word "GO," which was scratched on his body, and another was a scratch pointing to Roland's groin. Perhaps this indicated that the demon would leave by urination or excrement.

Roland seemed to fall into a quiet sleep, and during this period of time, no scratches appeared on his body. Father Bowdern and Father Bishop continued the prayers, alternating back and forth. When the Fathers began the Prayer to St. Michael, Roland instantly became violent by banging his fists on the headboard and then onto his pillow with extreme force. In the diary, Father Bishop described the action like "sparring." The family stated that they had not seen such a violent reaction from the boy until that night. Holy water was sprinkled upon the boy and he came out of his apparent sleep. When asked what he had been doing and what he saw, Roland responded by saying he was fighting a huge red devil. He stated the devil felt slimy and was very powerful. He spoke about being at the top of a very hot pit that was about one hundred feet deep. The devil was preventing him from getting through an iron gate at the top of the pit. He felt as if he could fight the devil, who was also surrounded by other smaller devils. When the exorcism prayers continued, Roland fell back into the "tantrum stage," and after a short time of deep breathing, he began to battle with the devil, who was trying to keep him down in the pit.

From midnight onward, it took two men to hold Roland down onto the bed as he tried to fight the devil. He would strike anytime he was able to get an arm free, with powerful blows beyond the normal strength of the boy. He spat at them and called them names. However, he used no vulgarity. The priests brought Roland back to a wakened condition by throwing holy water onto him. However, as the night wore on, it became harder and harder to keep him from the horrible sleep where he would endure "violent gyrations." It was

5:00 a.m. on the 17th before the boy went into a moderate sleep. According to the diary, Roland would be awakened at times with heavy eyes and each time he would ask for a glass of water, claiming he needed it because of the intense heat coming from the pit. The night ended with an apparent sleep episode where Roland began to sing such songs as "Swanee" or "Ol' Man River" in a high pitched, extremely loud singing voice. During these periods of song, the boy became calmer. There were only a few instances where he had to be restrained. While he was singing, his muscles would become relaxed and he would become very composed. He would also wake on his own without being slapped or the use of holy water. Around 7:30 a.m. on the 17th, Roland slept peacefully. He slept until 1:00 p.m. in the afternoon on that day and woke to eat a good meal and play a game of Monopoly. The first night of the exorcism had ended.

The description of Roland fighting with the devil in a pit of fire is quite a common occurrence in possession. Throughout the centuries, nightmares have been reported as a part of the demonic or diabolical attack. From a personal perspective, I can share with you these nightmares contain the most vivid and real imagery you will ever experience in a dream state. Even though one wishes to wake from the dream, it is impossible. The person who is going through this type of diabolical nightmare, or what the Church refers to as the nightmares of diabolical obsession, may demonstrate frightening displays much like Roland was. In this state, it is not at all unusual for the person to fight or even scream. It is very difficult to wake a person from this type of nightmare. Confrontation of some sort is often a reoccurring theme in the nightmare, much like Roland fighting his devil. In my 2010 book, *Crazy*, I devoted a whole section to discuss these nightmares and how they have related to almost every single real paranormal case I have worked on. It becomes quite apparent and irrefutable when you see this happening in case after paranormal case. There is something to this experience.

On his first night of exorcism, Roland is in a battle for his very existence. It seemed to me that once the boy was weakened from the battle, it was easier for him to be taken over by whatever was battling him. Once weakened, his body relaxed and he began to sing unnaturally. Could this be the point when the possession really begins to take hold on the boy? I believe what was witnessed was the battle for possession, and it becomes quite apparent with the entrance of the song state that the boy was losing his battle. I refer to this type of nightmare in *Crazy* like falling down a deep, dark hole—much like Alice fell down the hole in search of the rabbit in *Alice in Wonderland*. Things are different from that point on, and the battle becomes trying to find your way out of that hole. My friend Carmen Reed who's haunting was the basis of the film *The Haunting in Connecticut*, effectively describes this as being in a dark place. That is where Roland ended up in those moments. He was in a dark place with no hope of completely returning to a normal life. The possession had become completely transient, and that is why the next afternoon the diary states Roland enjoyed a meal and played a game. However, his attacker is not gone, and he is not normal again by any means. It is just a moment's reprieve of his struggle. French occult author Eliphas Levi effectively states, "When one creates phantoms for oneself, one puts vampires into the world, and one must nourish these children of a voluntary nightmare with one's blood, one's life, one's intelligence, and one's reason, without ever satisfying them." Eliphas explains the concept of writhing and it's correlation to paranormal experiences. In reference to Roland's experience with his entity, the writhing concept makes a great deal of sense. Roland was feeding his demons with his blood, life, intelligence, and reason. He fought with them endlessly, but could never satisfy their thirst.

Chapter 8
A Father's Love

There were times while I was living through the Union Screaming House Haunting when I felt I had reached a point of no return from the darkness. When those moments would happen, I would always feel a steadying hand upon my shoulder. I would turn to see that the steadying hand belonged to none other than my father. It was often followed with words of strength or encouragement. This was the way my father was throughout my entire life. Whenever things were too much to handle, he was always there with that steadying hand upon my shoulder. My father gave me the strength I needed to stand and fight for another day. He was strong for me during those difficult times in his own life. A great father supplies a steadying foundation for his child. I learned a lot about being a father and the strength it often takes to be one from my own dad. He was my foundation and the blueprint from which I put my own children back together after the horrible things life handed us when they were young. We see this sort of strength from Roland Doe's father.

Thursday, March 17, 1949-

According to the diary, Roland's father flies into St. Louis from Maryland and rushes to his bedside to be with him because of the escalation of events. This is really the first time in Father Bishop's diary that we get a glimpse of the relationship between Roland and his father. The simplicity of the moment is not lost within the diary, and I not only empathize with his father at this point, but he gains my instant respect. Roland's father drops everything when he understands that his child is in severe trouble. After the father settled in, both parents helped the boy change into his bed clothes around 9:00 p.m. They had difficulty keeping him awake long enough to get him dressed. Roland quickly fell into a deep "tantrum" sleep - the way he had the night before.

The boy went into the same type of violent fits. The father and the uncle had to forcibly hold him down onto the bed. With holy water and several hard slaps to the face, Father Bishop continued to bless the boy. The slaps indicated that the boy was completely out of control. The boy spat directly in the face of his father, mother, and uncle. His aim was precise, even with his eyes closed. During this whole ordeal, the boy's pulse remained steady and normal. There were no scratches on his body, but his actions were every bit as violent as they had been the night before. His threats were not vulgar, but were "loud and eerie." At times the boy would break into song. He would sing a line from "Swanee" in a high, loud, and off-pitch voice. The boy quickly fell into a deep sleep at 1:30 a.m. The priests left the house.

Just imagine for a moment you were the father of this boy. Imagine what it must have been like for this man to hold his out-of-control son down on the bed while being spat at and threatened. I cannot imagine what must have been going through this father's mind. You would like to think you can protect your children, but how do you protect them from something you cannot see and something you cannot completely understand? Where does that sort of strength come from in a man who sees his child literally falling apart? When we look at all the true cases of paranormal activity, we can clearly see the frightening aspects of each case, but there is much more going on than just horror. The true horror lies within the emotional damage being handed out in bushels to those living through these events. The father had to be completely falling apart inside, but in the middle of the violent attack on the boy, he had no time to deal with those feelings. You will do anything you can to protect your child from harm. We have all heard the stories about parents lifting cars and doing extraordinary things to protect their child. But what do you do when there is no car to lift and no door to break down? What do you do when you see your child at the point of insanity? In 1949, possession was a rare idea, and the occurrence in today's society is a little more understood, though still hard to fully comprehend.

Friday, March 18, 1949-

Roland went under once again. This time the father held the boy tight in his arms while the mother and aunt prayed the Rosary. The event lasted for almost an hour. This father is holding his child while this thing is ripping the boy apart from the inside out. I can almost imagine this father's jaw locked as he tries to fight back tears while his son fights beneath the tight hug of his arms. The instinctive action of the father is amazing. He turns to his love for his child. Love is not something the demon was looking or even hoping for as a reaction.

The demon wanted to make this child a monster on earth that everyone, including the priests, would look at with loathing. Instead the father grabbed the boy in his arms with love and held on for dear life. Love is a very powerful tool against the diabolical. The whole meaning of life and faith revolve around love.

The two priests, Fathers Bowdern and Bishop, along with Mr. Halloran, arrived at the house at 7:00 p.m. They sat around talking with the boy and playing games with him. This is a great indicator of the feelings these men were having toward the boy. It was not the result the demon was looking for. At 8:15 p.m., the boy retired to bed once again. The boy prayed the Rosary to the Virgin Mary with the priests present at his bedside, and they altogether recited the Novena Prayer to Our Lady of Fatima. This set the stage for the fathers to begin the Litany of the Saints, which is a series of petitions that would be recited by clergy and responded to by worshippers involved, as described in the Rite of Exorcism. The mattress began to shake with the boy still awake. The shaking ended with Father Bowdern blessing the bed with holy water. As the prayers of exorcism continued, the boy began to struggle with his pillow and his bed clothing. It took three men to hold him down at this point. They held his arms, legs, and head. The boy demonstrated enormous strength. He began to spit at the relics in the priests' hands. He started writhing with the sprinkling of holy water on his body. The boy screamed out in a high-pitched, diabolical voice. When he went through quieter moments, he laid with his feet moving in a rhythmical fashion. Father Bowdern would hold a Blessed Sacrament at one of the boy's feet and the movement would stop in that foot. Back and forth, the Blessed Sacrament would stop the moving of the feet. Father Bishop pointed out in the diary that "The manifestation of the power of the Blessed Sacrament showed up time after time again without fail."

As the exorcism prayers continued, Roland would go back into his tantrums even while he was trying to recite short prayers with Father Bowdern. At one point he stood on the bed and began to fight with everyone around him. Father Bishop described this in an entry, "He shouted, jumped, and swung his fists. His face was devilish, and he snapped his teeth in fury. He snapped at the priest's hand during the blessing. He bit those who held him." By midnight the boy began to change during the salaams. He stood up in the bed and then quietly fell to his knees throughout the salaams. As he bowed, the boy said, "Our Lady of Fatima pray for us," and he also repeated the words of the Hail Mary prayer. Then things begin to escalate once again as he began to beat a rhythm out on his pillow that sounded like the marching of horses. Then once again he rose up and "began his strong fight for the eviction of the devil." Then the boy writhed in all directions and he ripped off the top of his underwear and raised his arms above his head in a begging fashion. Then the boy began to gag. It appeared as if he was trying to raise the devil out of his stomach.

I have been a spectator during an exorcism when this occurred. In that case, the possessed person began throwing up a black substance while I held them. Beneath my arms I felt the bones of the possessed begin to move as the demon was expelled from the body through the most violent vomiting of this black substance I have ever witnessed before, and not since, in my life. I imagine this is what the boy was trying to accomplish on this particular night.

Roland asked for a window in the room to be opened, and seeming victorious, he said, "He's going, going,..." and then a moment later he said, "There he goes." He then fell limp onto the bed and in a moment he seemed normal and relieved once again. The family knelt by the bed with prayers of thanksgiving.

There is an important note made here in the diary: "The mother was beside herself." This is the first indication it would seem that the mother is really starting to be affected by what's happening to her son. She must have been dealing with tremendous guilt, and for the first time, I start to feel sympathetic toward her. It is important to remember that the possessed is often NOT the target of the diabolic. Many times in cases we see the child being attacked in order to get to one or both of the parents. Could it be that the possession finally had an impact on his mother? I would imagine there is a whole lot of truth in this statement. At this moment she may have come to the realization that the entity was not the dead aunt and that she was being duped by the demon. Now it was a fight for the soul of her child. Roland said he saw a huge cloud of black vapor in front of him. He said a figure in "black robes, cowl, and white (unintelligible) walked away in the cloud."

The descriptions of these events sound exactly like the occurrences during my own haunting, and they align with the cases I have worked with over the years. In the paranormal, the black vapor-cloud that Roland refers to is often called a "black mass." In fact, in one of the films I worked on for Syfy, we caught a black mass on film during the middle of the night in a very haunted wooden location.

As stated in the diary, Roland happily got out of bed and put on his bathrobe and walked to the door to see the priests out. It was 1:00 a.m. and the boy seemed to have made a complete recovery. The family and the clergy must have been relieved that this horrific ordeal was over. However, that feeling was very short lived because at 2:00 a.m., or a little after, the boy began to complain that he felt a strange sensation in his stomach. Shortly after, he began shouting in fear, "He's coming back! He's coming back!" At 3:15 a.m. the three exorcists were called back to the boy's bedside, but no further progress was made. At about 7:30 a.m. the boy fell into a deep natural sleep.

Chapter 9
Diabolical Escalation

One of The most noted exorcists of our time was the late Father Malachi Martin. "Exorcism can be extremely violent," he writes. "It is often disturbing, and always exhausting. I have seen objects hurled around rooms by the powers of evil. I have smelt the breath of Satan and heard the demons' voices—cold, scratchy, dead voices carrying messages of hatred. I've watched men writhing, screaming, vomiting, defecating, as we fought for their souls" (1992). There is a moment of escalation within possession, which usually follows a moment of reprieve. It seems the demon must surely be gone. There is a reason for this action, which is clearly part of the war tactics used by the demonic in spiritual warfare. Father Martin warns, "People are possessed in the way that dogs are infested. The demon does not physically inhabit the body; it possesses the person's will.

We have to compel the thing to reveal itself and its purpose. It can be slow and difficult, with the demon taunting, scorning, abusing you - speaking through the mouth of the possessed, but not in his or her voice" (1992). The next portions of the exorcism, according to Father Bishop's diary, illustrate the very things that Father Martin warns about.

Saturday, March 19, 1949-

The three exorcists arrive at Roland's aunt and uncle's house at about 7:00 p.m., and the exorcism begins at 8:00 p.m. when Roland is put to bed. On this night, violent shouting and fiendish laughter filled the house. According to Father Bishop, the shouting resembled that of a barking dog and Roland snapped his teeth, which seemed "truly" diabolical to the priest. The boy's violent reactions followed the prayers of exorcism. Then Father Bishop remarked on something I find very interesting, "There had been no violence from the boy before the exorcism was begun on the night of March 16." This refutes the accusation of the failed exorcism, which Father Hughes claimed was performed on the boy in a hospital in Georgetown. It would seem to me that if the failed exorcism actually took place in Georgetown, why was it not mentioned at this part in the dairy? Why would the family hide this failed exorcism from the three attending exorcists taking part in the exorcism in St. Louis? Father Bishop clearly states, "There had been no violence," preceding the starting of the exorcism in St. Louis.
It leaves you scratching your head and wondering why this failed exorcism was hidden—or did it even happen at all? It is truly one of the mysteries of the diary that creates more questions than answers.

The priests asked for a sign using the prayers of Praecipio on four different occasions that night. In response to this, the boy urinates uncontrollably. When the boy was awakened between those moments of transient possession, he complained that the urine was burning him. Remember Father Martin stating, "I've watched men writhing, screaming, vomiting, defecating, as we fought for their souls." This was clearly what was happening to Roland who, just before the urination began, woke up doubled over in pain and complaining that his stomach and throat hurt.

While under possession, the boy then began to sing in a very accomplished and beautiful voice. It is said that the "lala" section of the "Blue Danube" was sung with excellent and flowing gestures of interpretation. The other song he sang was the hymn "The Old Rugged Cross." Throughout the years, the attention has been on the evil in the cases of possession or demonic haunting. What is rarely ever discussed is the simultaneous presence of the Holy Spirit, the angelic - the good - that also surrounds the moment. When dealing with energy in the world, there is always a balance. The negative and positive energy in the atmosphere acts as a veritable yin and yang. Some speculate it may be God's way of demonstrating which path to follow. In my opinion, it is a direct indication that God is guiding the way toward salvation - a way out of an unlikely situation.

On this particular night, the boy demonstrated a skilled vice that reminded this group of people of the grace of God. This, of course, is in contrast to the previous night's events when the demonic spouted its ugly reverberations. It is also an indication to me that divine guidance was clear and present. It is important to remember that the supernatural can also be miraculous in nature. Up to this point, we have seen the boy act violently toward the relics and Blessed Sacrament. So why, then, would he begin to sing a clearly religious hymn in a beautiful, non-confronting fashion? Also, keep in mind there are moments when the demonic will retreat in order for the possessed to hold on to a crucifix or say a prayer. This is a tactic on the part of the demonic in order to try to convince the attending exorcist that the possessed is not possessed at all. In his 1992 book, *Hostage to the Devil*, Father Malachi Martin warns that he has seen the possessed hold on to a crucifix. This should not be considered by any means a sign that the exorcism is complete. It is just an indication that the demon is transient. This is also a positive sign because once the demon is no longer transient, the possession becomes what is known as perfect possession. According to Father Martin, "The most extreme state is 'perfect possession,' when the demon has taken complete control. The perfectly possessed person is totally lost. There is nothing I can do" (1992).

This is the ultimate danger - what the three exorcists were battling to avoid within Roland. They are trying to avoid the state of perfect possession, trying desperately here not to lose the boy and the salvation of his soul. The singing at this point is a reassuring sign of the positive presence of good and the fact the demon is still in a transient state. Interestingly enough, Roland could not sing and actually did not like to sing. It is mentioned in the diary that Father Bishop hummed the song *"Blue Danube"* while Roland was in a wakened state; however, Roland was unable to imitate the tune and also claimed he didn't even know the song.

But the boy still became vulgar in many ways. He also began threatening and admonishing the exorcists with vulgarity. During the night, what was described as a "playful call" was made to one of the priests. It was made in a sweet and pleasing voice, but when the call was ignored, Roland's voice became hard and it changed to, "Father you stink." This statement was followed by violence and fighting until Roland was completely exhausted and fell into a deep sleep. The time was 3:00 a.m. and the priests waited for a half hour before calling it a night.

Popular culture has brought major attention to demonic possession through film, TV shows, and print. However, it has also brought forth a lot of misconceptions and misunderstandings on the subject. As a society, when we think of exorcism, we picture the 1973 film, *The Exorcist*. As we work our way through the diary, we can see that some factual interpretations as well as dramatic interpretations were represented in the film. Don't get me wrong, possession is a horrible event where many frightening things can take place, which can and does have lifelong effects on the possessed and those exposed to the demon. Still, the reality of possession versus the dramatized version of possession is very different.

Even in documentaries concerning this case, the boy is perceived in a much different light than reality. It is also important to note that this over-dramatization often occurs because it can be hard to illustrate the possession due to the internal activities that are taking place in the possessed. It is also very difficult to communicate some events that may crucial in understanding the case, but on film, these events might be too subtle to understand. So instead, an artistic version of possession is demonstrated with the green skinned, glowing eyed, head spinning and screaming demon. It is important to note that even Father Martin acknowledges that our institutions are full of people who are possessed but have been simply misdiagnosed as schizophrenic. I think that is the one of the scariest and most frightening aspects of possession. Don't get me wrong, it is important for psychological evaluations to be completed in every suspected case of possession. It is when those evaluations are wrong that we lose people to a state that is next to impossible to recover from. Father Martin speaks of perfect possessions as people who can no longer be helped. Are these lost souls some of the individuals who are filling our psychiatric wards and institutions? The idea of this is more frightening than anything else within the realm of spirit or even the paranormal as a whole. What is even more frightening is the notion that a misguided and uneducated journey into the realm of spirit can be a possible cause of this type of possession.

Roland Doe could have easily have been sucked into this system and we may have never heard about him or his situation. The correct diagnosis for Roland was quite impressive. Professionals were able to observe him and determine that he was not suffering from a medical condition. It was very progressive thinking for a time period when people were being locked away in deplorable conditions without proper diagnosis or understanding. In order to understand the case at this point, you need to put aside the glorification of possession created by popular culture and see the case for what it is. It is crucial not to correlate Roland with the fictional Regan (from the 1973 film) in order to gain a solid understanding of what happened to this young boy back in 1949. It also helps to clarify and gain a clearer knowledge of what is happening to people around the world during what some might feel are these end times.

The Vatican itself is taking steps to put more exorcists into the field because of an alarming rise in possession throughout the world. This is not speculation. This is cold hard fact. Dr. Valter Cascioli, spokesperson for the International Association of Exorcists, told the *Catholic News Agency* in 2015 that demonic activity is "becoming a pastoral emergency. At the moment the number of disturbances of extraordinary demonic activity is on the rise" (Schneible). The *Catholic News Agency* also reported in this same article that Pope Francis said, "The devil exists and we must fight against him." Pope Francis is also paraphrased, mentioning "the battle against temptation is not with small, trivial things, but with the principalities and ruling forces of this world, rooted in the devil and his followers" (Schneible). Roland and the fictional Regan are very different given the reality of the modern world. When discerning the case of Roland Doe, we might find a truth which could be of value for all of us, Christian and non-Christian alike. This is not a Catholic problem. This is a spiritual problem for all of humanity. In the end we are all souls and we all suffer and grow from our human condition.

Chapter 10
On the Move

One time I had a minister express to me that he didn't believe in the type of paranormal work I'm involved in. I could not believe what I was hearing him say to me. How could a man of the cloth stand in front of me and say something so hypocritical? I looked at him with complete shock written clearly on my face, and I said as politely as possible, "Well that would make you one of the biggest hypocrites I have ever met. You stand at your pulpit every Sunday and you preach about the Holy Ghost and Jesus who himself is said by your teachings to have cast out demons. How can you possibly say that to me, and I will tell you one more thing, I have put more butts into church pews with the work I do than you could ever dream of doing." I walked away quietly, leaving him standing there with his mouth wide open.

The Bible is full of references to demonic possession. One of the most recited passages comes from the New Testament, Mark 5:1-15:

Then they came to the other side of the sea, to the country of the Gadarenes. And when He had come out of the boat, immediately there met Him out of the tombs a man with an unclean spirit, who had his dwelling among the tombs; and no one could bind him, not even with chains, because he had often been bound with shackles and chains. And the chains had been pulled apart by him, and the shackles broken in pieces; neither could anyone tame him. And always, night and day, he was in the mountains and in the tombs, crying out and cutting himself with stones. When he saw Jesus from afar, he ran and worshiped Him. And he cried out with a loud voice and said, "What have I to do with You, Jesus, Son of the Most High God? I implore you by God that you do not torment me." For He said to him, "Come out of the man, unclean spirit!" Then He asked him, "What is your name?" And he answered, saying, "My name is Legion; for we are many." Also he begged Him earnestly that He would not send them out of the country. A large herd of swine was feeding there near the mountains. So all the demons begged Him, saying, "Send us to the swine, that we may enter them." And at once Jesus gave them permission. Then the unclean spirits went out and entered the swine (there were about two thousand); and the herd ran violently down the steep place into the sea, and drowned in the sea. So those who fed the swine fled, and they told it in the city and in the country. And they went out to see what it was that had happened. Then they came to Jesus, and saw the one who had been demon-possessed and had the legion, sitting and clothed and in his right mind. And they were afraid.

I always find it amusing when someone tells me that they do not believe in demon possession. I immediately ask the question, "Do you attend church?" or "Have you read the Bible?" If the answer is yes, I immediately point out that according to their faith, they believe in the demonic. I can respect someone who says no to my questions because they cannot be held to a belief that they profess every single Sunday. The Bible is full of supernatural events and there is a whole sect of scientists and theologians out there who are on a constant search to bring a factual light to the stories of the Bible. If I were to say to a Christian, "Did you hear that they think the Shroud of Turin is authentic?" It would immediately begin a discussion on the reasons why it is authentic. However, when you pose that question to a non-believer, the discussion immediately turns to reasons why it might not be authentic. This is not the most perfect analogy, but you get my point. You cannot be of any faith and not believe in possession because it is part of every major faith known to man. It is something that you really need to sit down and decide for yourself. I cannot and will not tell you what you should believe. My place is to share ideas and theories for you to consider, and if somewhere within that self-reflection you figure out what you actually believe, then I have done my job properly. The answers lie within yourself, or in the case of possession, especially if it happens to you or someone you love. There is nothing that I can say to you to make you believe in something as non-concrete as the devil and possession. But keep in mind the age-old maxim that the devil's greatest trick was convincing the world he didn't exist. For all of our sakes, I pray we do not end up being the punch line of his joke on the world.

Monday, March 21, 1949-

Roland's family was getting very tired from the constant demonic barrage. So much so, his mother was sent to see a physician. This statement eludes that the effect the attack had on the mother had escalated. Father Bowdern felt that he needed to give the family a break and time to rest, so he arranged for the boy to be moved to Alexian Brothers Hospital, which is less than a half mile away from where I am currently writing this to you.

It was decided that in order to keep the boy's screaming from disturbing other patients, he would be put into a room away from the regular patients. The room that was chosen had the equipment needed to keep the boy in bed during his violent episodes. The boy was put to bed in the hospital room at 10:00 p.m. According to Father Bishop's description, Roland was frightened by the bars on the window, the straps on his bed and the knobless door to his room. This explains exactly where they put the boy in the hospital. He was obviously put into a psychiatric room. Father Bishop explains, "His whole reaction was of intense fear." Father Bowdern then began the exorcism with the Litany of the Saints, and when it was completed, everyone knelt in the room to pray the Rosary. The boy did not fall asleep then, as he had been accustomed. There was no apparent reaction from the demon. The three exorcists left the room while the boy's father remained reading prayers for him for about a half hour. What Father Bishop writes next is one of those striking moments within the diary, "One of the most edifying scenes since the beginning of the case was to see the father using prayers to get his son peacefully through the night." Father Bishop once again recognizes the loving nature of this father. The father spent the night on a divan in the same room, and when the boy awakened at 6:30 a.m., he was taken back to the uncle's house for the day.

Tuesday, March 22, 1949-

Roland went to bed at 9:30 p.m. at the uncle's home. What was intended as a day visit turned into an overnight situation. I would imagine it was due to some objection from the family to the hospital room's setup and the fear the boy showed toward it. Not long after Roland retired, the bed began to shake and it seemed the activity was beginning once more. Roland's mother immediately contacted Father Bishop and he and two other unnamed priests arrived at the house with the Blessed Sacrament about 11:00 p.m.

The three priests knelt at the bed of the boy and began the prayers of exorcism. The bed shook at three different points during the prayers. When they had completed the exorcism, the Rosary was recited and the boy fell into a natural sleep. The three priests left at midnight and there was no further disturbance the rest of the night.

Wednesday, March 23, 1949-

Father Bowdern arranged for the boy to stay at a room at the College Church Rectory. Two beds were provided in the room in order for the concerned father to sleep in the same room with his son. That evening, Roland took a brief lesson on the Catholic religion and went to bed at about 9:30 p.m. The Acts of Faith, Hope, and Love plus the Act of Contrition were recited by everyone in the room, including Roland. Immediately after Father Bowdern began the Litany, Roland went into his tantrum. Father Bishop tells us that the boy fought and kicked so hard that it was difficult to hold him down. The boy broke Mr. Halloran's nose and caused Father Van Roo's nose to bleed. His blows were quick and accurate even though his eyes were closed. When the exorcists reached the Praecipio, the boy began to urinate uncontrollably. When the boy came around, he complained of the same burning sensation as before. He urinated four or five times during that evening and passed gas three different times, which is common during a possession.

Things were getting ugly very quickly, and Roland became abusive and dirty. He said he met one of the fathers in hell, saying it was the year 1957. He seemed to be surprised by the presence of the father in hell. Father Bishop then writes, "The vile and filthy talk which followed makes anyone shudder." At one point, Roland pulls the towel from around his waist and begins to shake his body in a "suggestive and shimmy fashion." Father Bishop continues, "His expressions were lowly and smacked of the abuse of sex." In the years that followed the exorcism, it was reported that the majority of the priests who were witness to the possession felt that the boy had been sexually abused at some point in his life. In this modern age, with the world being brought closer together with social media and the Internet, it has made it much easier for those who have survived these extreme diabolical hauntings and possessions to communicate with each other and to compare experiences. In almost every case, researchers in the paranormal field have often discovered that some type of dysfunction is present before possession takes place. Could it be the boy was the victim of sexual abuse? Could that be the dysfunction that opened the door to the demonic in this case? This is entirely speculation, mind you, but there are some questions that arise due to Father Bishop's mention of sexual abuse. It is also important to point out that within these types of cases, many have complained of being sexually abused by the demon. Could Father Bishop have been pointing a finger toward demonic sexual abuse? The possibility is there for both scenarios. There is an indication from Roland that this is a possibility after he would complain that the men down there were using filthy language, especially since "Roland was never accustomed to filthy expressions in his regular life," according to the diary. Again, I think it is important to remind you that the year was 1949. This was a much simpler time and it would have been highly unusual for a young boy to be exposed to vulgarities, much less likely than it would be by today's standard.

The boy sang, barked, and contorted until he finally went to sleep at 2:30 a.m. It was mentioned that the boy was completely exhausted when he went to sleep.

In my opinion, I think Father Bowdern was doing what he felt was best for the boy by moving him to his uncle's house and the church rectory, especially since the hospital had a frightening effect on Roland. However, I do have to wonder if taking the boy to a church rectory somehow had a more violent effect on him than either of the other locations. Was the escalation due to the religious connotation of the location that he chose? Was it in the demon's plan, and Father Bowdern had just played into it? Either way, the choice of the location seems to have played a large part in the escalation of the possession when you stop and think about it. I am sure the father felt that the protection from a holy place might help Roland. We also need to understand that picking a location had to be difficult for the priest. Not only did he have the welfare of the boy to worry about, but he also had to find somewhere to house him. This would become increasingly harder in the days that followed.

Chapter 11
X Marked the Spot, or Did It?

Let's refer back to a passage scripted earlier on in the diary. This is an exact quote from Father Bishop's diary dated on March 16, 1949. Father Bishop writes, "To the question how many demons? A single line was scratched on R's right leg. There were at least four heavy brand marks in the form of an X."

Thursday, March 24, 1949-

What is described as the "reactions" began at the rectory at 9:45 p.m. and lasted until 2:30 a.m. Father Bishop believed that tonight would be the last night of the possession since it was the feast of St. Gabriel and the next day was the feast of the Annunciation. However, Father Bowdern disagreed because he had felt the "X" on the boy on the first night indicated the exorcism would last ten days. He believed that the devil would not leave until the next day.

At this point, I am going to make a few observations about the four X brands. I believe the X's were a direct answer to the question, which would have meant forty demons were present at that time. Also, interestingly enough, as a mockery of

God's word, the number forty could be a biblical reference to forty days and forty nights, among other biblical references.

The number forty is mentioned 146 times in the Bible. The number forty relates to a time of testing, trial, or tribulation. There are forty chapters in the book of Exodus. The prophet Jonah powerfully warned ancient Nineveh for forty days that its destruction would come because of its many sins. The number forty plays numerous roles in the story of Moses. Abraham tried to bargain with God not to destroy Sodom and Gomorrah if forty righteous people were found there (Genesis 18:29). The Bible was written by forty different people. These are just a few of the examples, and there are many more correlations to the number forty. This would make that number a perfect number for the demonic to use as a mockery of God.

It is important to understand that a demon will always lie. It was coming from the demonic, so why would the priests believe in what they were being told? I believe in some ways that this was a serious error on behalf of the exorcists present. They should have never listened to the demon in the first place. It's easy to be an observer on the other side of things while looking back at a case. What amazes me is that no documentary I've seen or book I've read on this particular possession correlates the number forty to a possible biblical mockery.

Thursday, March 24, 1949-

On that night, Roland demonstrated incredible strength. Father Bishop describes the scene, "Four men were holding him. R ran the gamut of shouting, screaming, barking, singing, kindly expressions, urinating, and passing foul air."

Roland told one of the fathers he would meet him in hell in 1957. He called the priest a big fat ass and an ox. The workman who was constantly helping Roland was part of his silly rhymes. "Michael, pickle, likel, sikel....Michael, you look so dirty." I have to wonder if the demon chose to tease Michael because of who he was, or if the demon chose Michael because of his biblical name, referencing Michael the Archangel? The demon would be repulsed by the name Michael because it is Michael who is called upon to battle the fallen.

The filthiest talk was spoken after midnight at the beginning of the feast of Annunciation. The boy began to use the foulest of language, which was sometimes sexual in nature. He yelled at the priests to "cut out the damned Latin ... Get away from me, you ... " followed by more vulgarity. At 2:00 a.m. the boy stated that all of the bystanders were going to stay with him until the end. Father Bishop writes "In a coy tone he remarked, 'You like to stay with me. Well, I like it too.'" The Blessed Sacrament had no effect on this boy during the night, and at 2:30 a.m. he once again fell asleep and slept until 11:30 a.m. the next day.

Friday, March 25, 1949-

Roland was still at the rectory and was very restless and could not sleep. A group of priests were praying outside the door of his room. For small periods of time, the boy fell into a restless and fitful sleep. On one occasion Roland fell out of his bed, but upon examination, it was observed he was not hurt. Next he walked awkwardly into the arms of Father Bowdern and Father Van Roo. Right before midnight, the boy lay on his back and began a sort of gymnastic exercise. There was no noise. After midnight, there was some moving around, but not for very long periods of time. He began cursing and spitting at his father. He also began kicking at the priests. He pushed the chair nearby his bed with his foot. At 1:00 a.m. he finally fell asleep. This was Friday night - the tenth night since the exorcism had begun. Father Bishop finally questions, "Perhaps the 'X' given on the first night was to mean 10 days?" On Monday night, Father Bowdern blessed the home and no disturbances occurred on Monday, Tuesday, or Wednesday night. Roland began to live a more normal life during these days. However, this normality was to be short-lived.

It appears that the exorcists were set up with the whole idea of ten days. The demon had obviously lied and then toyed with them using the boy as part of its plan. The priests had made a very crucial error in thinking and they played directly into the demon's hands. Even Father Bishop does not mention the significance of the error in the diary. It is quickly dismissed and forgotten as the diary moves onward. The appearance of the X's became an obsession for the exorcists. A demon will often present a riddle to be solved, but at the same time, that riddle can easily be turned into a joke on those who try to solve it. In this case, in order for this particular demon to carry out the punch line, he gave the priests a few days of reprieve—just long enough for everyone to relax and think they won the battle. I am sure during those days of serenity Father Bowdern felt he got it right, believing they were completely successful in solving the riddle and ridding the boy of the demon. However, this "happily ever after" was just part of the diabolical fantasy trap, which was set up for all of them. Once the trap was sprung, it was off to the races once more.

Chapter 12
The Meaning and Importance of Numbers in the Occult

Like anything else, it is important for us to look at the significance of numbers. The demonic will often utilize the meaning of numbers in a possession. We have seen this time and time again in popular culture and with the use of the numbers 666 within literature and films. Remember the mark of the beast found underneath Damien Thorn's hair in the film *The Omen*? This was fictional, but it does have its basis in biblical fact. Revelation 13:17–18 tells us, "And that no man might buy or sell, save he that had the mark, or the name of the beast, or the number of his name. Here is wisdom. Let him that hath understanding count the number of the beast: for it is the number of a man; and his number is Six hundred threescore and six." Numbers in the Bible are often found to have symbolic significance. When looking at the acts of Lucifer and his legion of demons, one must consider the significance of any numbers present in their messages. Numbers are just as important within the occult as they are in worship.

Let's take a look at a historical example. According to National Geographic's documentary *Hitler and the Occult* (2007), it is not a secret that

Adolf Hitler had a deep interest in the occult. He planned his actions very carefully around numbers and the alignment of planets and stars. Hitler carefully chose the date of his suicide, April 30, 1945, because it coincided with the first day of the Pagan spring holy days. According to the occult doctrine, Hitler chose to carry out his suicide at 3:30 p.m. This combination of threes represented the most favorable time to depart this life and re-enter the reincarnation cycle. The triple threes that are found present in the Hitler suicide are from the 30th of April, 3 o'clock, and 30 minutes past the hour. Hitler was engaging in typical occult behavior by arranging the timing of his death in a very precise, numeric manner. It has been theorized that Hitler wanted to exit this life at such a proper time in order that he could come back quickly, as the real Antichrist. Once you understand the importance of numbers in the occult, what Hitler was attempting according to his beliefs was a very well thought out plan.

After considering Hitler's suicide as an example, we can now analyze the importance of numbers in the 1949 Exorcism Case. Roland Doe was given five days of rest and respite. What does the number five mean first biblically, and secondly, what does the number five represent within the occult? The number five is mentioned 318 times in scripture. Its biblical meaning has to do with God's grace and favor toward humans. I find this interesting because it may have been a message that good was prevailing. A time of rest - with the corresponding number of five - could have been an indication of God's favor toward Roland. However, on the other hand, the number five in the occult is the number of light. To understand this implication we need to look at the name given to the devil in the Bible, Lucifer. Lucifer is the name in Latin meaning Lucem, which means bringer of light. I have seen this reference to Lucifer as the bringer of light in other demonic cases throughout my career. It is possible that Roland was given the five days of rest specifically in praise of Lucifer and as a mockery of Father Bowdern's belief that the boy would be spared after ten days. The number five goes into ten twice, which could have been an indication of a complete mockery of the priest and God's grace and word.

Thursday, March 31, 1949-

At 11:30 p.m., Roland came downstairs in his uncle's house and complained that he was feeling ill and that his feet were going cold and then hot. The family went back upstairs with him, and that is when the disturbances began again. The shaking of the bed started and then Roland began to write on his bed sheet with his finger, claiming that he was writing what he was seeing on a blackboard. The family in the room was unable to make out what he was writing on the sheet until Roland began to talk, telling them what he saw on the blackboard. What follows are the direct notes from Father Bishop's diary that were written down by Roland's cousin.

I will stay 10 days, but I will return in 4 days.
If XXXXXXX stays (gone to lunch).
If you stay and become a Catholic it will stay away.

XXXXXXX
God will take it away 4 days after it is gone 10 days.
God is getting powerful.
The last day when it quits it will leave a sign on my front.
Father Bishop—all people that mangle [sic] with me will die a terrible death.

The family called Father Bowdern at the rectory at about midnight, and Father Bowdern along with Father Van Roo arrived at the uncle's house at about 1:00 a.m. At that time, Father Bowdern once again started the Rite of Exorcism. During the Praecipio, Roland requested a pencil. At the beginning of each one of Roland's spells, he would address two people: "Pete" and "Joe." He began to write on the head of the bed, which was covered in a white cloth. "This type of spell and writing was repeated eight or ten times." What he wrote was recorded for the most part in Father Bishop's diary. The following is the list of writings taken directly from the diary.

In answer to the first set of questions he wrote the Roman numeral X. (It was clearly the numeral, with crossbars at the top and bottom). This was written four times on this first occasion and was repeated several times during the exorcism, usually in answer to the question, "diem."

I will stay 10 days and then return after the 4 days are up.

I am the devil himself. You will have to pray for a month in the Catholic Church.

(In answer to the command to give "nomen lingua Latina.") *I speak the language of the persons.* (Word language was misspelled.) *I will put in XXXXXXX's mind when he makes up his mind that the Priests (sic) are wrong about writing English. I will, that is the devil will try to get his mother and dad to hate the Catholic Church. I will answer in the name of Spite. In 10 days I will give a sign on his chest he will have to have it covered to show my power.*

He drew a strange thing that looked somewhat like a map, with *"2,000 ft"* written on it (apparently connected with early dreams about hidden treasure and a map to find it). I believe that it was in this connection that he spoke also, saying "Yeah, that is what I got on the Ouija board." He drew a face also, and wrote the words: *"Dead bishop."*
You may not believe me. Then R will suffer forever.

When commanded to give a sign in Latin, he wrote meaningless marks on the paper, not even letters of the Roman alphabet.

We need to take a closer look at the numbers ten and four, which are beginning to make continued appearances in the boy's writings and sayings. In a biblical sense, the number ten is a perfect and complete number that signifies testimony, law, responsibility, and the completeness of order. The number ten has the strongest occult pulls of all the Hebrew letters. Ten is the number of karma, good or bad, depending on the actions of the person involved. I do not think it is mere coincidence that the demon is choosing to depict ten in the form of Roman numeral X. We see the X in the tarot deck as the Wheel of Fortune card, meaning "what goes around comes around." It could also be a karmic symbol. The possession was the end result of behaviors and actions of the boy and his mother. Also keep in mind that a treasure map was mentioned. Was this map in reference to the dead aunt's hidden money that the family was searching for? One important thing to note is the boy said he was told about the "2000 ft." and the map through the Ouija board, which he had been no doubt using with his mother. The number ten, or the X, is now referring to the karmic price I believe the mother and the son are paying for their actions.

The number four is directly related to creation. On the fourth day, God created the universe - the stars, moons, and planets, which help to tell time. Four could be considered a reference to time. There are four beasts in Revelation and there are four Archangels, including Michael. There are four different types of elementals within the occult. The zodiac has four stationary winged signs. There are four seasons. Four is a powerful number of creation and time. Man has four evil tendencies: evil inclination, evil thoughts, evil words, and evil actions. In my opinion, the number ten and four together are indicating a karmic price that needs to be paid by evil itself.

The demon will confuse and lie. What I find interesting is the fact that no one has looked into the meaning of the numbers besides signifying literal days. Much like 666 is the mark of the beast, these numbers mean something other than the number of days. The demon is selecting them carefully and with purpose. It is almost as if the demon is toying with them by providing them the answers, knowing they will misunderstand them. The answers are being given, but the clarity to interpret those answers is completely missing.

Chapter 13
Baptism and Communion

Martin Luther said, "Baptism is no human plaything but is instituted by God himself. Moreover, it is solemnly and strictly commanded that we must be baptized or we shall not be saved. We are not to regard it as an indifferent matter, then, like putting on a new red coat. It is of the greatest importance that we regard baptism as excellent, glorious, and exalted" (*Large Catechism* 4:6). Luther's words illustrate the importance of baptism within Christianity. The question that seems to come up time and time again, a question that is no different in this case, is: "Is it possible for someone who has been baptized to become possessed?" The answer to that question in an absolute, hands down yes. Keep in mind that in the first stage of demonic possession, the affliction is awakened by someone who knowingly or unknowingly invited them into their lives.

There are definitely opposing views when discussing who can become possessed. There are some who might disagree with me when I say a Christian cannot be possessed. However, I would have to make the argument that there is a difference between a "true" Christian and one who is less than true to the beliefs they profess. Simply put, you cannot claim to be washed in the blood of Christ and then turn around and practice things that are prohibitive in biblical and Christian teachings. I would argue this not only makes you a target, but it paints a bull's-eye on your back. In some ways I think it is even worse to have once been a Christian and then turn your back on your beliefs. In an article for *Christianity Today*, Marshall Shelley poses a great question: "Can a Christian be demon-possessed?" That question produces lots of disagreement among theologians. Most would say that a believer probably couldn't be totally possessed, but they might experience some form of oppression (or very strong influence) by demons. The Bible does describe followers of God coming under the influence of evil spirits - King Saul disobeyed God's instruction, and the Bible says, "The Spirit of the Lord had departed from Saul, and an evil spirit ... tormented him" (1 Samuel 16:14, NIV). Judas, the disciple who betrayed Jesus, was possessed by Satan (Luke 22:3). And an evil spirit influenced Ananias and Sapphira, husband and wife, to lie to their fellow Christians and to God (Acts 5), leading to their deaths. It is possible, according to scripture, for God to step aside and let oppression and possession happen to someone who claims to be Christian. Living a life according to Christian beliefs is also essential for protection from diabolical forces.

I use to have a friend who was a minister and would often say, "I cannot be possessed by a demon because I am possessed by the Holy Spirit." There is some truth to that statement. However, when you stop letting the Holy Spirit move within you, then you become vulnerable to demonic attack, and as we have seen in scripture, it is even possible for God to step aside and let that attack take place. So, the question then becomes, "Once you are lost, how can you find your way back into God's grace?" Through the regeneration and the purification of your soul, and one of the easiest ways to accomplish this is through Christian baptism. One of Father Bowdern's wisest moves was to insist Roland be baptized as a Catholic.

Friday, April 1, 1949-

The diary explains Roland had been taking Catholic instruction from Father McMahon since March 23. It is apparent Roland wanted to become Catholic because the diary tells us his father and mother wanted to leave his choice of religion up to him, and because of his choice, they agreed he would not be confirmed Lutheran, as previously planned. (Roland had already been baptized in the Lutheran church, but confirmation always follows baptism in the Lutheran faith.) During the five days of solace and what the diary calls "respite," it was agreed the boy would be baptized into the Catholic Church.

So, the sponsors were picked and the baptismal party was supposed to arrive between 8:00 and 8:30 p.m. at St. Francis Xavier College Church. As they drove from the uncle's house to the church, Roland began to complain he was feeling a strange sensation in his feet that would alternate between a cold and hot feeling. Roland went into one of his spells in the car. He began saying, "So you are going to baptize me! Ha! Ha! - And you think you will drive me out with Holy Communion. Ha! Ha!" Roland grabbed the steering wheel of the car and the uncle had to pull over in order to subdue the boy. It turned into quite the struggle. Roland stiffened and fought. It was next to impossible to get him out of the front seat of the car and into the back. The uncle and father were trying to hold Roland down in the back seat while the aunt drove, but even with the two strong men holding him, Roland still managed to lunge at his aunt behind the wheel. The radio, which was playing fine in the car, stopped playing during his fit, only to be working completely fine afterward.

At the college church rectory, another struggle made it difficult for three men to carry the boy from the car inside. Inside the door of the rectory the boy began shouting and spitting. Because of his violent outburst, the men had to throw him on the floor. Even dousing him with ice cold water had no effect on him. He left his father and his uncle completely exhausted from his battle with them. Roland was taken up to the third floor of the rectory where he was placed on a bed. It was impossible for the baptism to take place at the baptismal font, as planned with the sponsors. So instead, the workman, Michael, was chosen as a proxy and the baptism began on the third floor of the rectory.

Seizures took over the boy's body off and on, not leaving enough time for the profession of faith and abjuration of heresy. Seeing this, Father Bowdern had Roland repeat the words in a shorter and briefer form. Understanding it was next to impossible to continue in the normal fashion, Father Bowdern turned to using the procedure for the baptism of infants. When Roland was asked if he renounced Satan, he went off into one of his spells. Roland was not able to say the words to renounce Satan.

Finally, Roland entered into a normal state long enough to give the answers to the questions asked of him by Father Bowdern. When the priest came to the baptismal prayer, the boy went into a "physical resistance," which is said to have exceeded any other violence of the evening. Roland remained conscious for the words, *Ego te baptizo in nomine Patris*. Upon completion of this phrase, there was a "violent upheaval." Father Bowdern however had completed the baptism with an abundance of holy water. At this point, Father Bishop tries to answer the same questions we asked earlier, "It seemed from the reactions that the Lutheran baptism had not been administered properly, or that it had not taken effect." The prayers of exorcism continued after the baptism with the same type of violence, spitting, and gyrations that had been seen on previous occasions. It continued until about 11:30 p.m.

With the baptism completed, the next step would be to give the boy his first communion. However, can a possessed person take Holy Communion? Exorcist Father Jose Antonio Fortea states, "Yes, it is not only licit but also quite necessary. In moments of crisis, the demon moves the body of the possessed even while possession does not diminish liberty. It is therefore that a possessed person may confess and be in God's grace" (Barillas). Why would Holy Communion be an important act for Roland to partake in? Monsignor William P. Fay explains the importance of Holy Communion.

Jesus gives himself to us in the Eucharist as spiritual nourishment because he loves us. God's whole plan for our salvation is directed to our participation in the life of the Trinity, the communion of Father, Son, and Holy Spirit. Our sharing in this life begins with our Baptism, when by the power of the Holy Spirit we are joined to Christ, thus becoming adopted sons and daughters of the Father. It is strengthened and increased in Confirmation. It is nourished and deepened through our participation in the Eucharist. By eating the Body and drinking the Blood of Christ in the Eucharist we become united to the person of Christ through his humanity. "Whoever eats my flesh and drinks my blood remains in me and I in him" (John 6:56). In being united to the humanity of Christ we are at the same time united to his divinity. Our mortal and corruptible natures are transformed by being joined to the source of life. (2001)

It is apparent that the reason Father Bowdern turned to Holy Communion as the next step was to strengthen the power of the Holy Spirit, which was brought into Roland's life through his baptism. This is an essential part of the Father Bowdern's arsenal to fight the demons within Roland.

Saturday, April 2, 1949-

Roland awoke around 9:30 a.m., but he was far from being calm. He broke a light by throwing his pillow at it. He also shattered the crockery basin in his room. This is the day that Roland was scheduled to receive his first Holy Communion. Father Bishop and Father O'Flaherty assisted Father Bowdern with the preparations. "It was evident that the struggle was at hand," Father Bishop writes in the diary. Roland had no difficulty going through the "conditional" confession. Perhaps the boy's quietness was a sign the baptism from the day before had taken hold.

When Father Bowdern began speaking the prayers for the Holy Communion, Roland went into a spell, keeping his eyes shut and his mouth closed. Each time the Eucharistic particle was placed into Roland's mouth, he would spit it out. For nearly two hours they attempted until Father O'Flaherty suggested they pray the Rosary in honor of Our Lady of Fatima because it was, after all, the first Saturday of the month. After praying the Rosary, the priests once again attempted to serve Holy Communion to the boy. Finally, with "extraordinary opposition," Roland was finally able to swallow and take his first Holy Communion.

After taking the Holy Communion, Roland dressed to go home. It was about 11:45 a.m. when they left for the uncle's house. Father O'Flaherty was driving with Father Bowdern and Roland's father with Roland sitting in the backseat of the car. After being on the road for only a few minutes, Roland jumped and grabbed Father O'Flaherty and had to be pulled off of him by force. Roland showed signs of normalcy only a few times during the whole trip.

Once back at the house, Roland was able to eat a "good-sized' breakfast. However, he was only conscious for brief moments during the rest of the day. Father Bishop states, "The sacraments had stirred up Satan more than any other priestly administration." Not only was the family nervous from the long day of fighting, but they were also completely worn out. Fathers Bowdern, Bishop, and O'Flaherty along with Michael, returned to the house at 7:40 p.m., and Roland's tantrums continued. During the Praecipio, there was no response before 8:40 p.m. There was one short spell that lasted less than a minute between 8:40 p.m. and 11:40 p.m. "During this period R ate a dish of ice cream." Father Bishop writes in the diary.

Roland ran downstairs at 11:15 p.m. and sat on the arm of a parlor chair. He could no longer stay in the confines of the bedroom because he was becoming so nervous. Father Bowdern, who was afraid Roland would get violent, asked him to return to the bedroom. Roland boyishly trotted up the stairs and went into the bedroom and ran straight to the reliquary of the holy cross. Father O'Flaherty caught Roland's hand in time, but Roland reached for the open ritual and tore four pages out of the exorcism formula. "He grasped with lightning speed," Bishop wrote. Roland then went into one of his spells during which Father Bowdern asked the boy to respond in Latin to the Praecipio. Roland's only responses were to repeat the Latin words and respond with a remark of "No" or a laugh of ridicule.

The same type of responses to the Praecipio continued at 12:15 a.m. The diary goes on to explain, "There was a jumbled mockery of the Latin questions." At this time, writing appeared on the boy's body. "The letters GO were printed in red as they were on the first night of the exorcism. At the command '*dicas mihe tiem,*' three parallel scratches appeared on R's thigh. At '*horam*' an X was branded. Three [unreadable] were branded on different parts of R's body," according to the diary. At 1:15 a.m., Roland became so nervous that he wanted to sit in a chair beside the bed. His hands nervously trembled. Then he began begging his father to take him back to Washington because he feared he might be going crazy. Natural sleep finally came to Roland at 1:40 a.m.

The Blessed Sacraments were causing an escalation in the boy. It seems as if an internal spiritual war was going on inside him. The constant nervousness is also an indication of this internal battle. Everyone must have felt like they were failing the boy because the baptism and Holy Communion seemed to have made things worse. It is also very sad that the boy stated he was afraid he might be going crazy. One of the major things a demon will try to do is make you second-guess your sanity. They will also make those around you second-guess your sanity. Demons would like nothing more than to make society believe that mental illness is the catalyst behind the possessed person's behavior. The devil wants to deceive and to destroy man. He uses truth mixed in with his lies. He will use this misguided knowledge in his favor. Once the possessed begins to question their sanity, it becomes increasingly harder to fight because the question then becomes, "Who am I fighting? Am I fighting with myself and my own mind?" Make no mistake; this is a very dangerous state to be in. This is when thoughts of suicide and acts of self-mutilation and self-harm come into play.

Sunday, April 3, 1949-

At 7:00 a.m. Roland woke up and threw his pillow at the ceiling light and then went back to sleep. He had a short seizure at 8:30 a.m. and then went back to sleep again. Upon waking at 11:30 a.m., he ate breakfast. Roland went downstairs at twelve noon. There were several spells during this time but nothing of a serious nature. At 4:00 p.m. Roland began playing a game of ball with his father, two uncles, and a cousin. At one point, the boy threw a ball to his father and began to "stagger as a drunken man."

Witnessing that Roland was behaving strangely, his father ran to Roland to help him. Roland then ran with his eyes shut, at a high speed and in a straight line, through two of the neighbor's yards. It took three men to catch him and carry him back home. Later on during dinner, Roland lifted the kitchen table up with one of his legs. He ate very little supper. At 7:00 p.m. Fathers Bowdern, Van Roo, Bishop, and O'Flaherty arrived at the house. Within a few short moments of their arrival, Roland grabbed at his aunt and almost tore her dress, but several men came to her assistance. Roland fought the men as he was carried upstairs, but he quickly came back into himself when he was thrown onto his bed.

The fathers hoped that God would put Roland out of his suffering on this night because it was Passion Sunday. The fathers began the exorcism, and this time there was no response at the Praecipio. Roland began shouting and singing in rhythm with a devilish prophecy regarding his little cousin. He continued this over and over for around ten minutes. "You will die tonight. You will die tonight." The only way to quiet Roland was to put "a pillow in his face." From 9:30 p.m. until 12:00 a.m., there were no disturbances, other than the sound of the boy snoring and his restless sleep. The fathers left the house. However, trouble began once again at 12:30 a.m. Roland's arms were bound with tape and gloves were placed over his hands. He complained that the adhesive from the tape was hurting him and that his hands were getting hot inside the gloves, but as soon as the gloves were removed, he became violent once again. He did not fall into normal sleep until 3:30 a.m.

On this night, we see the demon lying in order to cause chaos. Stop and imagine what it must have been like for the young cousin to hear that "You will die tonight," over and over in the taunting, singing rhyme? Consider the distress this must have caused for the aunt, the mother of the young cousin. When you look at this night of the possession, I see the demon for some reason trying once again to get to the aunt. It is almost as if she is paying the price for taking them to the church and for the ultimate success of the baptism and the boy's first Holy Communion. The aunt is attacked in the car on the way to the church. She is attacked again on this night when Roland grabs hold of her and almost rips her dress. The taunting of the younger cousin would appear to be an attempt to get at the aunt. There might be some- thing more here than what Father Bishop knows or is telling us. It may even be that the aunt was becoming the weak link in the family structure. It appears the demons might have been targeting her for some reason. Was her faith weakening? Was it becoming too much for her? There is something more going on inside of her than what is revealed by the diary. There is a reason the bull's-eye is placed on her on this night. Whatever that reason is will remain a mystery; however, it is an important thing to point out.

Many times we only think of the possessed and what effects they're enduring, but we cannot overlook the importance of the attack on the others present. The possession plays into everyone involved on multiple levels as a result of implanted thoughts and emotions, lack of sleep, loss of appetite, stress, and much more. Spiritual warfare encompasses every single person. It even plays a role with me as I write these very words and with you as you read them. Saint Pope John Paul II once said, "'Spiritual combat' is another element of life which needs to be taught anew and proposed once more to all Christians today. It is a secret and interior art, an invisible struggle in which (we) engage every day against the temptations, the evil suggestions that the demon tries to plant in (our) hearts." He was speaking about all of our hearts, including yours too.

Chapter 14
Going Home

Monday April 4, 1949-

Father Bishop writes in the diary that arrangements have been made to take Roland back to Washington, DC, by train, which departs St. Louis at 9:30 a.m. This change of plan is interesting. First, Roland's father had already missed so much work, which is understandable under the circumstances. Second, the family they were staying with was becoming too strained. The attack seemed to have an effect on more than just the immediate family. Fathers Bowdern and Van Roo accompanied the parents and the boy on the train. This is the first time Father Bishop has even mentioned the mother since her obvious breakdown early on.

In order to wake Roland up for the trip, cold water had to be splashed on his face. His father, mother, uncle, and a friend of the family accompanied Roland to the railroad station. Roland boarded the train with no difficulty. He walked and chatted normally with everyone. On the train to Washington, DC, Roland had no problems at all except one short period of violence occurring when he retired at 11:30 p.m.

I have to question the decision to take the boy on this long trip home by train. With the different types of things that were happening to him, they were taking a huge chance by not only traveling but traveling with him on public transportation. Any number of things could have happened on that journey. It also seems that the clergy were not worried about the other passengers being exposed to Roland on the train. What if during one of his spells he was able to get away and injure himself or one of the passengers? It was an unwise move that should have been met with a lot resistance from the exorcism team. Everyone was extremely fortunate the demonic did not decide to cause one of many worst-case scenarios.

Tuesday, April 5, 1949-

They woke Roland on the train and he was taken to his home in Maryland without any incidents occurring. During the morning, Father Bowdern met Father Hughes (from the early days of the case) at St. James Church in Mount Rainier, Maryland. During that visit, Father Bowdern found out that Father Hughes had made arrangements through the chancellor of the Archdiocese of Washington, DC, to continue with the exorcism. The pastor of Roland's previous congregation at St. James Church wanted to take full responsibility of the case, but there was a lack of room for the boy. All who were concerned felt that Roland should not be kept at this home. Fathers Bowdern and Hughes contacted several hospitals in Washington, DC, but because of the nature of the case, none of them were willing to accept the burden.

Wednesday, April 6, 1949-

Father Bowdern and Father Hughes went to Baltimore to find a room at an institute there. The

Daughters of Charity were willing to give Roland a room, but the staff doctors felt that since the case was not a psychiatric case, it was not something they could do. Besides that, the hospital was dependent on the state of Maryland for aid because each patient had to be accounted for on record. It would have been exceedingly rare to include the treatment of exorcism. Extremely disappointed that they were being turned away in both Washington, DC, and Baltimore, Father Bowdern once again turned to his friends at the Alexian Brothers in St. Louis. He called St. Louis and spoke with Brother Rector Cornelius, who promised Roland a room. That entire day went well for Roland, and he even exercised in the afternoon. That night when he went to bed, there was a very short spell, but it could have been a nightmare.

Father Hughes is again mentioned in Father Bishop's diary without noting the supposed exorcism attempt at Georgetown University Hospital. As a matter of fact, it becomes quite obvious that no one in the Washington, DC, or Baltimore area wants to even touch the case. This is the boy's hometown, and it must have been very frustrating for Father Bowdern to be unable to find a place for the boy, even within his own parish. Was the previous exorcism by Father Hughes just another myth in a long list of myths about the boy and his possession? There is just not enough within the diary to point to this previous exorcism ever happening. We are left scratching our heads as to why it is never mentioned.

One of the best explanations behind the alleged exorcism at Georgetown University Hospital comes from Father Joseph Jenkins, pastor of Holy Family Church in Mitchellville, MD. Father Jenkins writes,

*The priest, Fr. E. Albert Hughes, went to the
chancellor of the archdiocese. He was warned to
move slowly and not to leap to rash judgments. The
young priest explained that he had done as much.
After a meeting with the archbishop, Most Reverend
Patrick A. O'Boyle, he was authorized to initiate the
exorcisms. Fr. Hughes resisted, hoping that an
older and more experienced man might be chosen
instead. He understood that this should be done by
a very holy man because the devil wants to expose
the sins of the priest; so the Father went to
Baltimore and made a general confession.* (2014)

Father Jenkins goes on to explain that the
exorcism took a wrong turn. According to the
eyewitness who may have confessed to Father
Jenkins, Jenkins was drafted to assist Father Hughes
in the exorcism of Roland Doe when he was moved
to Georgetown Hospital. The eyewitness was a
young man who served in the church and was asked
to assist due to his size and strength. The eyewitness
said that even he had a hard time holding the boy
down during the attempted exorcism. He said that
Roland was able to spit across the room and at one
point he lost his patience and even slugged him to
keep him under control. The witness acted as the
priest's bodyguard. Apparently they tied the hands
and feet of the boy to the bedposts and he reacted
violently, causing loose items to fall to the ground.
Roland possessed incredible strength and vigor.
Father Hughes warned his assistant not to enter into
any conversation with the boy, but to only give the
required responses to the ritual prayers from him.
Roland began to speak Aramaic, a form of ancient
Hebrew. Previously, the boy had been harassing
them in Latin. The boy growled and broke free from
his restraints. He somehow tore through the
mattress and ripped out a metal spring. Father
Jenkins adds, " ... At the conclusion of the Lord's
Prayer, the boy attacked the priest and tore a gash

into the cleric's arm from his shoulder to his wrist. Blood exploded over everything! The ritual prayer book was caked in the priest's blood! He screamed out! The exorcism had ended in failure. Father Hughes' life was saved by the doctors, and his arm had a long track of a hundred plus stitches. He would have lingering problems with the arm and it would visibly drag at the consecration during Masses."

After the failed exorcism, Father Hughes supposedly made the eyewitness go to confession. He was advised to share the evenings events with no one, not even is mother. One thing to note within this passage is that there was an eyewitness who was still living at the time of this writing, which was in 2014. I do want you to keep in mind that the eyewitness account sounds very much like numerous testimonies that have been given throughout the years by Father Halloran, who assisted Father Bowdern in the 1949 Exorcism Case - even down to the point of the boy spitting and Father Halloran losing patience and striking the boy. Also, it seems to me that it would have been impossible for Father Hughes to hide his injury from others. However, the question still remains why this previous exorcism was never mentioned in the diary. Keep in mind Father Bowdern personally spent time with Father Hughes. Surely, this information would have been shared between the two fathers trying to help the boy. Even Father Jenkins seems to question Father Hughes' strength of faith and his ability to offer a complete confession. This is not an unusual argument. Maybe it is this argument that Father Bishop was trying to spare Father Hughes from, along with his obvious failure to complete the attempted exorcism. Perhaps Father Bishop was extending a professional courtesy toward Father Hughes by excluding this information from the diary. It will remain a mystery of the case.

Thursday, April 7, 1949-

It was another normal day for Roland. He was doing so well that he was able to do a little gardening outside. He spaded and then cut the lawn throughout the afternoon. However, that evening Roland went into one of his spells that lasted from 9:15 p.m. until 2:15 a.m. During that night's exorcism, at least twenty different brands appeared on the boy's body. Roland was awake for the branding. Many of the brands appeared at the name Jesus as he was reciting the Hail Mary. The first brand was a number four. Other brands could have also been the same number, but they were not clear. Several times four claw marks or scratches of varying lengths would appear on his belly or legs. Shockingly, a pitchfork appeared. One set of claw marks appeared from his thigh to his ankle, which tore off a scab that was near his ankle. The boy's hands were being kept away from his body as these marks appeared. One branding appeared on his leg as he was beginning to lie down. Almost all of the branding occurred under his clothes or under the sheet that was covering his body. Roland became very violent again and began spitting. He began to sing and hum "Ave Maria." He spoke with what Father Bishop described as filthy talk. He then began writing on his own body by scratching the words into his flesh with his own fingernail. He scratched the words "HELL" and "CHRIST" in large capital letters onto his body. The devil spoke through Roland saying he would keep the priests until 6:00 a.m. He made this statement at 2:00 a.m. when everyone was already worn out. He said he would prove this point by having four awaken immediately. At 2:15 a.m. Roland went fast asleep.

It was felt by Father Bishop that God had permitted Roland to fall asleep to spare him.

Friday, April 8, 1949-

It was a quiet and routine day for Roland. However, as the night went on, a five-hour session of spells took place. It began when Roland was alone in the bathroom. There were 135 minutes "of great physical violence." Father Bishop described the events of the night.

This continued with shorter spells until 1:20 a.m.: violence, spitting, nonsense jumbling of Latin questions, singing "Blue Danube," "Ave Maria," and so forth. There was filthy talk and movements and filthy attacks on those at the bedside concerning masturbation and contraceptives, sexual relations of priests and nuns. Irritated and impatient after the long struggle, Fathers Hughes and Canning arrived with the Blessed Sacrament about 11:00 p.m. The house was blessed by Father Hughes. R twice threw a pillow in the direction of the Blessed Sacrament. He took one sedative, spat it out, and then finally swallowed it.

This night concluded Roland's visit home; the next day began the journey back to St. Louis.

Let's visualize for just a moment what the boy's appearance looked like at this point. The effects of sleep deprivation on his appearance would have been horrifying. His eyes would have been sunken and red. Dark circles would have resonated from his eyes. The body would show signs of the constant stress and malnourishment. Then there is the issue of the brandings and scratches all over the boy's body. Roland's body would be covered with them at this point. Twenty of these brandings and scratches happened in one night. Not only would they be unsightly, but they would have also been painful as well. Just stop for a moment and consider the horror of his appearance. It is impossible to not sympathize with this child when you stop to really con- sider what he might have looked like from the abuse of the possession and the utter agony and pain of his experience.

Chapter 15
The Devil Rages While the Faithful Pray

On Saturday, April 9, 1949, Roland began his return trip to St. Louis where he had been prearranged to stay at Alexian Brothers Hospital. The trip was fairly uneventful with nothing more than a slight disruption when the boy went to bed for the night.

Palm Sunday, April 10, 1949-

It was the start of Holy Week when Roland arrived back in St. Louis and was immediately taken to Alexian Brothers Hospital. He was taken into one of the brothers' private living rooms for the day. At 7:00 p.m. Bowdern, Bishop, O'Flaherty, and Van Roo arrived at the hospital. Roland was given the same room from his previous visit on the fifth floor. They prayed the Rosary several times and the exorcism was completed without any incident. At 11:00 p.m. Roland fell into a "good" sleep. At midnight, the fathers decided to wake up the boy in order to give him communion. Roland was having a very hard time staying awake for more than a few seconds at a time. But - in this section of the diary there was a portion missing. Father Bishop says, "When the -" and the page ends there. It is picked up with Father Bishop talking about an experiment they were trying in order to wake the boy long enough to take communion. It continues with Father Bishop saying, "[The] Fathers were planning to abandon the experiment, R became quite normal and was able to receive Holy Communion without special effort. He settled back on his pillow with a smile and was soon in deep sleep. Nothing disturbing happened throughout the night."

Monday, April 11, 1949-

Brother Emmett kept Roland busy by giving him different sorts of manual work to be done on his floor at the hospital. It was Brother Emmett's way of making friends and of gaining Roland's confidence. It also helped Roland to better understand his psychiatric surroundings, which in return helped make them more agreeable for him as well. At 8:00 p.m. that night, Bowdern, Bishop, Van Roo, and Mr. Halloran arrived at the hospital. Father Bowdern brought Roland some Catholic readers and some other stories for him so he would have more than just his catechism to read and study. At 9:00 p.m. Roland went to bed and the exorcism was completed. Father Bishop wrote, "The evening gave every reason for expecting quiet." However, when the fathers were praying the Rosary, Roland felt a "sting" upon his chest. Only a blotch of red was noticeable at this time. The Rosary was continued and Roland felt a more severe branding upon his chest. Father Bishop explains, "The letters were in caps and read in the direction of R's crotch. 'EXIT' seemed quite clear. On another branding, a large arrow followed up the word 'EXIT' and pointed to R's penis. The word 'EXIT' appeared at different times in three different parts of Roland's body." He felt horrible pain in his kidneys and in his penis and would cry from the burning sensations. He complained of even more severe pain every time he urinated.

Father Bishop continues in the diary, "At midnight, the Fathers planned to give R Holy Communion, but Satan would have no part of it." Roland's body became severely scratched and branded as the fathers were explaining to Roland the institution of the Blessed Sacrament. The word "HELL" was printed on his chest and thigh. As the attempt at Holy Communion continued, long heavy scratches appeared on Roland's hips to his ankles in clear protest. When Father Bowdern tried to give Roland a small particle of the sacred bread, he went into a seizure and the devil proclaimed he would not allow the boy to "receive." It was thought at this point that a spiritual communion would have to be administered. But the words, "I want to receive you in Holy Communion" were cut off at the word "Communion" with a seizure. It seemed that administering the Eucharist would stir the devil up even more than it ordinarily did that evening. The usual routine of barking, spitting, cursing and fighting continued longer than it usually did. There was no quiet sleep on this night even with the devoted fathers continuing to pray.

The clergy praying for this boy to find peace throughout the night paints a powerful picture. Their utter devotion to not only the child but to God goes without question. It must have been a struggle to focus on the evil in the boy day in and day out. It is so easy for us individually and collectively to forget that evil exists in the world - on our streets and even at times within our own home. One of the most dangerous spiritual actions you can take is to deny the existence of the diabolical in all of our lives. I am not saying to live your lives in constant fear of the devil. I think in today's world there is too much attention being paid to him anyway. I find the dichotomy funny: on one hand the world seems mesmerized, fascinated, and even entertained by the works of Satan and his minions, but on the other hand the majority of people want to believe he does not exist at all. The overall "fallacy diagnosis" of someone affected by the diabolical is either insanity or mental health issues. Ironically enough, Aleister Crowley writes in his book *Magick: Liber ABA: Book Four* that "The sin which is unpardonable is knowingly and willfully to reject truth, to fear knowledge lest that knowledge pander not to thy prejudices" (1998). He is saying that man's greatest sin is to ignore truth because it does not fall into a box he is comfortable with. I would argue that attempting to understand that which makes us uncomfortable is most important when dealing with the truth of the spiritual realm. Now mind you, Crowley was also the one who said, "One would go mad if one took the Bible seriously; but to take it seriously one must be already mad" (1998). Obviously, the Bible was not pandering to Crowley's prejudices. However, we see this same attitude in belief among Christians as well. In "Demons: Ancient Superstition or Historical Reality?" Wayne Jackson, MA writes "Certainly Satan exerts great influence today. However, as God does not work miraculously in this age, but influences through his Word and through the events of providence, so also, the devil wields his power indirectly, and non-miraculously, through various media. Current cases that are being associated with demon possession doubtless are the results of psychosomatic problems, hysteria, self-induced hypnosis, deception, delusion, and the like. They have natural, though perhaps not always well-understood, causes" (1998). This is a complete denial of the possibility of demonic possession within a Christian understanding, which seems to me to not only be misleading but a dangerous attitude as well.

On the other hand, there are many psychiatric professionals throughout the world who would tell you that demonic possession is alive and well within our psychiatric institutions. Dr. M. Scott Peck, psychiatrist and best-selling religious author, describes exorcism in our mental facilities today in his book, *People of the Lie*.

When the demonic finally spoke clearly in one case, an expression appeared on the patient's face that could be described only as satanic. It was an incredibly contemptuous grin of utter hostile malevolence ... Yet when the demonic finally revealed itself in the exorcism of this other patient, it was with a still more ghastly expression. The patient suddenly resembled a writhing snake of great strength, viciously attempting to bite the team members. More frightening than the writhing body, however, was the face. The eyes were hooded with lazy reptilian torpor - except when the reptile darted out in attack, at which moment the eyes would open wide with blazing hatred. Despite these frequent darting moments, what upset me the most was the extraordinary sense of a fifty-million-year-old heaviness I received from this serpentine being. It caused me to despair of the success of the exorcism. Almost all the team members at both exorcisms were convinced they were at these times in the presence of something absolutely alien and inhuman. The end of each exorcism proper was signaled by the departure of this presence from the patient and the room. (1998)

I have personally met psychiatric professionals who would tell you there are events happening within institutions that go without explanation or understanding. At this time, Roland was being housed in a psychiatric ward with the ability to confine and restrain him when needed. It makes you wonder how many people are currently in the same predicament that Roland was in. How many people are out there in institutions being drugged and restrained into some form of submission? At what point does the possession take you into the realm of insanity, never to be brought back from the nightmare again?

Chapter 16
Holy Week

Holy Week is the most important week of the Christian year. It begins on Palm Sunday with Jesus triumphantly entering Jerusalem. On Maundy Thursday, Christians give remembrance to the Last Supper and the betrayal of Jesus by Judas Iscariot, his disciple. Good Friday is the saddest day of the Christian year with the observance of Jesus dying on the cross. Easter Sunday is the end of Holy Week with the celebration of the Resurrection. This is a very busy week for clergy.

When putting Holy Week into perspective, biblical scholars, theologians, priests, and others have often warned we should never look upon those who played a part in the Passion of Christ as evil. Condemning them is a clear mistake and one that is not only wrong but also ill conceived.

Judas was living his life and doing what he thought was best just in the same way Pilate and Caiaphas were taking part in what they believed was their role in life. They did not see themselves or their actions as playing into the devil's master plan or even God's master plan, for that matter. This is reassuring when you think about all that is diabolically evil in the world. We need to understand where and how we participate with that evil in order to conquer it. I think this is the hardest part of helping someone with a demonic haunting case. It is hard to make someone admit or even understand their role in an event they feel like they are the victim in. You cannot change things about yourself unless you acknowledge your involvement in the first place. Humanity as a whole continues to make the same mistakes time and time again. All the blame does not lie in the demon present in your life. Somehow, somewhere, an invitation was made in order for the diabolical to breech the faith of an individual. Step one in the stages of possession is called "invitation" for a reason.

The role of Judas in the betrayal of Christ has been a debatable topic in recent academia. An ancient codex, or book, was found that dates back to the third or fourth century AD. The book is known as the Gospel of Judas. It was discovered in Egypt in the 1970s and was written in Coptic or Egyptian Christian; it is believed to indeed be a translation of the original text. The text has been eighty-five percent restored, but there are still gaps that remain.

According to Stefan Lovgren in a 2007 article for *National Geographic News*, "The author of the text is unknown. But scholars say it originated with a group of early Christians known as Sethian Gnostics. These 'heretics' believed that truth could be known only through revelation from Jesus and a personal experience with God - hence the Gospel of Judas's subtitle: 'the secret account of the revelation that Jesus spoke in conversation with Judas Iscariot.'"

April DeConick, a professor of biblical studies at Rice University states, "He emerged as a much more negative Judas - a demon Judas as evil as ever" (Lovgren). The article for *National Geographic News* goes on to explain that DeConick began analyzing the text immediately after it was published last year, but noticed her translation wasn't matching *National Geographic's* in significant spots. The debate starts when Jesus calls Judas *"daimon." National Geographic* maintains that daimon means "spirit." DeConick, however, argues that daimon should be translated to mean "demon," and that Jesus literally calls Judas a demon. "What we find in all the Gnostic materials - and I've found about 50 references to the word 'daimon' in these text, is that, they're always indicating demons, malicious figures that possess and torment people, trying to get people to do things they're not supposed to do against God," DeConick said (Lovgren).

Anneliese Michel was a young German girl who, in her early twenties, was visited by the Blessed Virgin who asked her if she was prepared to suffer greatly for the German youth and priests. The source of this suffering would be demonic possession. The film, *The Exorcism of Emily Rose*, is loosely based upon her true-life story. According to the Blessed Mother, Anneliese was to be a victim soul who would show the German people and the world the devil does really exist. There are some who believe she should be sainted for her sacrifice. During her long ordeal of possession, she was able to go to mass, say the Rosary, and was able to receive the Blessed Sacraments.

It is believed that she was possessed with up to ten demons, including Cain, Nero, Judas Iscariot, Valentin Fleischmann, Hitler, Legion, Belial, and Lucifer. The question has always been, was she actually possessed by those listed? Were all of these demons? Or was she possessed by the demons that had possessed these people to perform their evil deeds? Also, the fact she mentions Belial in particular is interestingly in correlation to the St. Louis case - I will share more on this with you later. In the recording (this was the first case of possession and exorcism that was recorded on tape), there was some evidence that suggests Judas is indeed a demon. In *Anneliese Michel: A True Story of a Case of Demonic Possession*, the priest's questioning provokes Lucifer to say, "I took Judas with me! He is always at my service. He is damned. He could have saved himself, but he has not followed the Nazarene" (Fortea and LeBlanc). Judas also speaks when questioned, "I am damned for eternity! You careless people, if you could just imagine what it is to be damned for eternity! I am damned!" Judas had another very interesting thing to say about the modern age: "These modernists are the result of my work and they already belong to me." These two statements add credence to the suggestions in the Gospel of Judas that Judas was or is now a demon. He is clearly damned for eternity, especially since he speaks of the results of his work concerning the modernists.

On July 1, 1976, Anneliese Michel died at her home. The autopsy *reports* her death was the cause of malnutrition and dehydration. She had been in a semi-starvation state for almost a year. She weighed only thirty kilograms (sixty-eight pounds) on the previous day, and she had two broken knees from the continuous genuflections under possession. Anneliese was also reported to have had pneumonia.

The exorcism began on September 24, 1975. In all, she had been subjected to sixty-seven exorcisms until her death. Her parents were prosecuted for negligent homicide. The verdict was that the priests would be fined and no one would serve time in jail. Her parents were set free because they had "suffered enough." This is a truly controversial case. However, regardless of anything that has been written about Anneliese Michel - from those who were present to the Vatican itself - all you have to do is to listen to the tapes of her while she was under possession to understand there was indeed something supernatural going on.

The 1949 Exorcism Case and the Anneliese case have many aspects in common. One of these aspects is the mentioning of the name Legion. According to now deceased Father Halloran, who was around twenty-eight when he participated in the exorcism of Roland Doe, "During the rite when it was asked its name the only answer I can remember that was given was 'Legion,' which reminds us of the swineherd running into the lake" (Brown). In Mark 5:9, Jesus is asking the demon to reveal itself in much the same way the exorcists have done in both of these cases.

Holy Week is a time to remember Jesus's sacrifice, but it is also a time to remember evil and how it can work inside each of us, in the same way the demons were currently working within Roland Doe. When asked, "What were the most striking physical phenomena that you witnessed yourself during the exorcisms?" Father Halloran replied to the question,

I think the markings on the boy's body. I didn't think there was any way they could have been self-induced, the marks, the scratches, the words, the numbers, and that sort of thing that appeared [in blood red]. When the evil spirit took over the child, there seemed to be nothing he could do about it. There were a couple of times when something very dangerous might have happened and he had no recollection whatsoever of anything that took place when he was in one of these sieges. And that affected me, the power that someone or something has over someone. (Brown)

Tuesday, April 12, 1949-

Right after the exorcism prayers began, the activity started up. While the fathers prayed the Rosary, the violent performance began again, but this time the markings weren't being made on the boy's body. Everyone was disturbed by the noise and singing. Roland gave no responses to the Praecipio. He would laugh, imitate the Latin words, or he would just simply say, "Stick it up your ass." The devil decided to show his power through Roland. He told those present that he would have the boy awaken "pleasant and attractive." He kept his promise and Roland woke in the manner that was spoken. A few minutes passed and the devil said he would have the boy awaken and this time he would be "offensive." Roland woke very irritable and he complained quite "bitterly" to those who were holding him. Several unsuccessful attempts were made to give Roland Holy Communion, but the devil stated he would not let the boy have it. Quiet sleep followed around 1:30 a.m.

Wednesday, April 13, 1949-

Roland took Holy Communion in the morning without any trouble. That afternoon Mr. Halloran (before he was a father) took the boy to the White House retreat. Father Halloran describes this event later in an interview with *Spirit Daily*, *I took him out to the retreat house in St. Louis, a very pretty place, to get out of the hospital and get some fresh air, and he didn't know anything about the Stations of the Cross and so I asked if he wanted to learn and he says, oh sure. He was an affable little kid. Not many 14-year-olds would say they were interested in finding out about the Stations of the Cross, but he was. And I explained what each one signified and we got to the 12th station and I said, this commemorates Christ dying on the cross and with that he took off and ran toward the edge of a bluff that dropped down about 150, 200 feet down to the tracks and I hollered at him and nothing happened so I ran and for once in my life I made a decent tackle* (Brown).

Father Bishop in the diary states it happened at the fourteenth station. He also states that the spell lasted for twenty minutes and Roland had to be carried back to the car.

At 8:45 p.m. that evening, Roland was ready for bed. He happily played with trick gadgets that Father McMahon had given to him. While sitting on the bed, he had a quick but very violent seizure. This was before any prayers had begun for the evening. The exorcists thought that it would be an important evening. Roland spoke almost immediately in the voice of the demon and told them that God had commanded the demon to leave at 11:00 p.m. that very night and that he would not leave without a struggle. He proved his point that night by showing more physical power than had ever been previously shown before. The first spell lasted for twenty minutes - Father Bowdern was in the middle of the exorcism and the brothers were praying the Rosary. During the Praecipio, Father Bowdern, who had always insisted the responses be in Latin, remained persistent in his demands. The devil responded in pig Latin, imitated the commands back to the priest, or used the vulgar expression, "Stick it up your ass." He began singing the words, "Stick it up. Stick it up." At this point in the case, the devil had never once answered in Latin, but his imitation of Latin was sharp and precise.

The vulgarity and "damning" threats to those at the boy's bedside continued as before. The arrival of a new nuisance was the loud shouting of "Fire!!" At 10:45 p.m. He began to make the noise of a church bell sounding the 11:00 p.m. hour. He made a "bong" sound, but would hold on to the "ng" sound at the end of the word. The church bell sounds continued after the passing of the 11:00 p.m. hour, and it became evident that everyone had been deceived by the devil's statements at the beginning of the evening. After midnight came Roland could not take Holy Communion and would go into immediate spells and would not even be able to say the word Communion. Again, Satan stated that he would not allow the boy to take Holy Communion. At this time the Brothers were performing round the clock adoration of the Blessed Sacrament. By midnight they had been praying for several hours and they had completed a large amount of Rosaries. Father Bishop wrote, "Their prayerful assistance is worthy of the highest comment."

April 14 to 16 of 1949-

Through Holy Thursday, Good Friday, and Holy Saturday, no disturbances occurred according to Father Bishop's diary. The thought was that it was due to a new statue of Our Lady of Fatima, which Brother Rector purchased and had placed on the first floor corridor of the hospital. The statue was dedicated to the Blessed Virgin with petition to Our Lady of Fatima and would intercede for Roland in his ordeal. The brothers promised Our Lady of Fatima community devotions if the boy was to be spared from his possession. Father Halloran spoke about an interaction with the boy on Holy Thursday in an interview with *Spirit Daily*, "But I wondered why me, what purpose I was there for. There was one time he asked us to stop and took his pajama top off and he was covered with these marks, scratches, and he said they hurt. It was Holy Thursday and I was telling him about Holy Thursday and he started writhing around in pain and he said, look, I can't stand this. He seemed more affected when I said things like 'the Blessed Sacrament' or mentioned the ordination of priests and things like that" (Brown).

On Good Friday, Roland listened to the Tre Ore Services on WEW, a radio station. Brother Rector bought a small colorful statue of St. Michael the Archangel on Holy Saturday. The statue was placed in Roland's room. Father Bishop wrote, "It should be remarked here that one of the most effective prayers of exorcism was that dedicated to St. Michael." On Saturday night it was decided that Roland would be awakened at 6:30 a.m. for Holy Communion, and he would then attend the second mass in the brothers' chapel on Easter morning.

Easter Sunday, April 17, 1949-

Father Widman, the hospital chaplain, made three unsuccessful attempts at giving Roland Holy Communion in his room. Father Bishop wrote, "After some waiting and slapping of R the fourth attempt succeeded." Now Brother Theophane was on nurse duty in Roland's room. He was reading the Office of the Blessed Virgin. He came to the "Regina Caeli" at about 6:45 a.m. when Roland jumped out of the bed and grabbed the Office book from the brother. Roland reached for the scapular that was on the brother's habit on a nearby chair. Roland fought the brother and spat at him while trampling the scapular with his feet in an Indian war dance. The devil said, "I will not let him go to Mass. Everyone thinks it will be good for him." Because of his frequent seizures, it was impossible to get him to the chapel for mass. They called

161

Father Bowdern and shortly after he arrived to the hospital the spell was broken. Everything remained calm until that evening.

That evening, Roland was able to spend a little bit of time with the brothers outside the hospital. Brother Emmet was taking Roland back to the basement floor of the hospital when he began to fight violently. Brother Emmet called out to the other brothers for help but it took a long time for them to hear and get to him. He was completely exhausted from the whole struggle. Roland was again taken to his fifth floor room in the hospital. The prayers of exorcism began immediately with the usual struggles and violence. The devil once again decided to show his power over Roland by saying he would have him awaken and ask for a knife. He was threatening to kill those who had molested him while he was in his seizure. When Roland came out of the spell, he asked for a knife in order to cut an Easter egg. A little later the devil said he would awaken Roland and he would ask for a drink of water. Roland woke and carried out the devil's plan. There was nothing but taunting remarks to the exorcists during the Praecipio, and no responses were given. Everyone was becoming very tired of the long performance, including Roland himself. Roland did not fall to sleep until midnight and the fathers left the hospital at 12:45 a.m.

Chapter 17
Dominus

Who is St. Michael the Archangel, and what is his role within the ritual of exorcism? According to the *Catholic Encyclopedia*, "St. Michael is one of the principal angels; his name was the war-cry of the good angels in the battle fought in heaven against the enemy and his followers" (Holweck). St. Michael in mentioned a number of times in the scripture:

Daniel 10:13 sqq.: Gabriel says to Daniel, when he asks God to permit the Jews to return to Jerusalem: "The Angel [D.V. prince] of the kingdom of the Persians resisted me ... and, behold Michael, one of the chief princes, came to help me ... and none is my helper in all these things, but Michael your prince"

Daniel 10:12, the Angel speaking of the end of the world and the Antichrist says: "At that time shall Michael rise up, the great prince, who standeth for the children of thy people."
Apocalypse 12:7, "And there was a great battle in heaven, Michael and his angels fought with the dragon."

The prayer to St. Michael during the exorcism ritual is as follows:

In the Name of the Father, and of the Son, and of the Holy Ghost. Amen.

Most glorious Prince of the Celestial Host, Saint Michael the Archangel, defend us in the conflict which we have to sustain against principalities and powers, against the rulers of the world of this darkness, against the spirits of wickedness in the high places. Come to the rescue of men whom God has created to His image and likeness, and whom He has redeemed at a great price from the tyranny of the devil. It is thou whom the Holy Church venerates as her guardian and protector; thou whom the Lord has charged to conduct redeemed souls into Heaven. Pray, therefore, the God of Peace to subdue Satan beneath our feet, that he may no longer retain men captive nor do injury to the Church. Present our prayers to the most High, that without delay they may draw His mercy down upon us. Seize the dragon, the old serpent, which is the devil and Satan, bind him and cast him into the bottomless pit, that he may no more seduce the nations. ("St. Michael the Archangel")

It is important to remember what Father Bishop wrote, "It should be remarked here that one of the most effective prayers of exorcism was that dedicated to St. Michael." This prayer is effective because when we speak of spiritual warfare, we call upon St. Michael to protect us in battle. He is the guardian and the protector. He defeated Lucifer, and it was his name the angels screamed as a war cry during that battle in heaven.

Monday, April 18, 1949-

The morning was very violent with Roland completely out of control. Father Bishop writes about that morning in the transcribed passages that follow.

8:00 a.m. - R woke in a spell, kicking at the brother at the bedside. He jumped out of bed, seized the holy water bottle, threatened to throw it at the brothers, and then sprinkled the water toward them. Finally, he threw the bottle over their heads, smashing it against the ceiling.

8:15 a.m. - Father Widman attempted to give R communion. It was impossible. Spitting: unable to even make spiritual communion: Made one spiritual communion. The devil then seized him and said that one devil was out, and that R had to make nine communions (sacramental or spiritual apparently) and then he would leave his body. R continued for an hour unable to make spiritual communion or to receive the Sacrament.

10:00 a.m. - There were more spells when attempting spiritual communion. R was able to say: "I wish to receive you" (That is all the priest attempted to have him say since it was sufficient). The devil laughed and said: "That isn't enough. He has to say one more word, one little word, I mean one BIG word. He'll never say it. He has to make nine communions. He'll never say that word. I am always in him. I may not have much power always, but I am in him. He will never say that word." Several spells: violence, singing, urination.

11:30 a.m. - R said he was very hungry, and wanted a bath and food. We put him off until noon. Then gave him a tray: cake, ice cream and milk. R threw the glass against the wall, scattering broken glass all over. Violence intermittent until about 1:30 p.m. R was very discouraged and disgusted and mean.

During the afternoon, the brothers brought Roland a tray of chipped beef, which they had arranged on a small table in his room. Roland picked up the plate and ran over to the window and held the plate in an almost "perpendicular" manner, daring the brothers to come closer. Even though the two brothers tried to get to him, one went under the bed to grab his feet and the other headed toward him to restrain his arms, the plate was still thrown against the opposite wall. Father Bishop wrote, "No one was hurt but the plate was broken to bits."

The fathers created their plan of attack that evening on the way to the hospital. It was agreed upon that Father Bowdern would ask for the responses to be given in English during the Praecipio. Even though Roland might protest, the medals were to be left on his body and a crucifix was to be placed in his hand every time he went into one of his spells. These things were decided on because of information gathered from several other cases of possession.

At 7:00 p.m. Fathers Bowdern, Bishop, and O'Flaherty arrived at the hospital. Father Van Roo had spent most of the day with Roland but had just been relieved by the brothers before the evening meal. Roland asked if he could make a telephone call to his mother, but on the way to the telephone, he went into one of his spells and had to be forcibly carried back to his room, "in a fighting mood."

Father Bowdern was reading the Rite of Exorcism quietly, and when he came to the words, "*Tu pax confirmes, Tu fiscera regas,*" he blessed Roland with the sign of the cross. Almost immediately, Roland repeated the words back to the priest and asked what they meant. He repeated in Latin several times. The sign of the cross and the crucifix seemed to work. But when they tried to force the crucifix into his hand, Roland became very violent. In one instance Roland threw the crucifix out of his hand. Then Father O'Flaherty began teaching Roland the "Ave Maria" in Latin because the boy was showing an interest in learning Latin, and in a very short time, he could repeat most of the prayer back perfectly. Roland paid close attention as Father O'Flaherty told him the story of Our Lady of Fatima. Roland then asked for a Catholic reader that contained eigth-grade prose and poetry. He sat in his bed thumbing through several stories. Afterward, behaving like a young boy, he began balancing the book on his knees and also on his head. Roland went into one of his spells while the book was balanced on his knees and immediately the book went flying across the room. Roland was in and out of seizures between 9:30 and 10:00 p.m. The most impressive prayer of the evening was Roland's Rosary. At this moment, the boy demonstrated remarkable reverence.

Father Bishop wrote that Roland was more cooperative on this night that he had been ever before. During those times when he was "out of seizure" the boy felt that he needed to be praying. He asked if he could make spiritual communions on his own, and he wondered if he could bring on his spells through his prayers. Every single time he was out of a spell, he went into prayer. After each of the spells, he claimed that the light was getting brighter. The light he was speaking of seemed to be at the end of a dark tunnel. He complained that the medals around his neck were getting very hot and he wanted to take them off, but he was not allowed to do so. During one of his spells, Father Bowdern forced a reliquary crucifix into his hand. Father Bishop wrote, "The reaction to the medals and the crucifix was exceptional." When Father Widman blessed Roland with his ordination crucifix and asked Roland to kiss it, the boy went into another one of his spells. During the Praecipio, Father Bowdern asked the responses be given in English as was planned on the way to the hospital that night.

He was given responses back in Latin. While Father Bowdern used the Praecipio, Father Bishop recited the exorcism prayer over and over.

At 10:45 p.m., the most striking event of the evening happened while Roland lay calmly during one of his seizures. A clear commanding and dignified voice broke into the prayers:

"Satan! Satan! I am Saint Michael, and I command you, Satan, and the other evil spirits to leave the body in the name of Dominus, immediately. – Now! NOW! N O W!"

Then came the most violent contortions of the entire exorcism. "Perhaps this was the fight to the finish," Bishop wrote. Father O'Flaherty and the brothers were physically sore and exhausted from the fight. Roland fought for seven or eight minutes, and then in a tone of complete relief, he said, "He's gone!" Roland went back to normal and told everyone present that he felt fine.

Roland described what he saw. I am going to give the complete quote from Father Bishop's diary for this description.

He said there was a brilliant white light and in that light stood a very beautiful man, with flowing, wavy hair that blew in the breeze. He wore a white robe that fitted close to his body. The material gave the impression of scales. Only the upper half of the body of this man was visible to R. In his right hand he held up a wavy and fiery sword in front of him. With his left hand he pointed down to a pit or cave. R said he saw the devil standing in the cave. R felt the heat from the cave and saw the flames. First the devil fought, resisting the angel and laughing diabolically. Then the angel smiled at R and spoke, but R heard only the one word "Dominus." As the angel spoke, the devil and about ten of his helpers ran back in the fire of the cave or pit. After the devil disappeared the letters "Spite" appeared on the bars of the cave. As the devils disappeared into the pit R felt a pulling or a tugging in the region of his stomach. As the devils disappeared, he felt a snapping, and then felt relaxed completely. He said that this was the most relaxed feeling he had since the whole experience began in January. R related his visual experience at 11:00 p.m. This time was approximate to the time that the manifestations of the devil began in Cottage City, Maryland, on the evening of January 15, 1949.

After midnight, Roland led a Rosary with the fathers and brothers responding. He was completely relaxed, comfortable, and normal. Arrangements were made that Father Van Roo would say a mass for Roland at 9:30 a.m. on Tuesday morning in the hospital chapel. Roland woke up Tuesday morning, April 19, 1949, and was taken to the chapel, where he then attended his first Holy Mass since becoming a Catholic. He took his first Holy Communion while kneeling at the alter rail with no difficultly whatsoever. Since Monday at 11:00 p.m., there were no more indications that the devil was present. Roland had been successfully exorcised.

August 19, 1951-

Father Bishop's diary gave a follow-up stating, "On August 19, 1951, R and his father and mother visited the Brothers. R, now sixteen is fine young man. His father and mother also became Catholic, having received their first Holy Communion on Christmas Day, 1950." This ends the explanation of events that are described and outlined in Father Bishop's diary.

Chapter 18
Keeping the Secret

Father Bishop's diary ends the story of this case in 1951. However, the message of this case reaches far beyond Bishop's diary. The story does not end or begin with the diary. The diary is the most complete timeline of events in existence. With that being said, there are many more questions about the events of 1949 that remain unanswered. Throughout the years, the urban legends surrounding this case have overshadowed the truth of what happened to Roland Doe. There are many locations, details, and secrets that have covered up the truth. In the beginning I think the idea was to protect the boy and his family on the part of the Church.

Roland Doe

The continual life-long victimization of Roland is the authentic story. Roland Doe was not a monster. He was a little boy who is now an old man and living a full life of his own; he has feelings just like the rest of us. His feelings are something that have long been ignored, and now he has been molded into something to be feared. The books, the films, and the articles always seem, in one way or another, to be placing the blame on Roland, always trying to find fault in "the haunted boy."

I have read a slew of reports that paint Roland as a horrible, uncooperative child. There have even been reports that referred to Roland as possibly being homosexual. While the fault is misplaced on Roland, there seems to be a strange, overwhelming sympathy for all the adults involved in this case. In reality, the adults were the true monsters, not Roland. His real identity should have been protected, and it should have never been allowed into the public arena. It is said that he has no memory of the events that transpired. I would tend to believe that is an attempt on his part to avoid further public scrutiny and a media frenzy that would surround him if he ever decided to come forward with an interview. The truth is, most likely there are things that he does remember quite vividly. He may not remember everything it its entirety, but he most likely is haunted by memories of at least part of his experience.

One of the reasons I refuse to use his actual identity is because I do not want to play into the feeding frenzy that must haunt this man's life. Can you imagine what it must have been like to grow up as the "Exorcist Boy"? He must have been horrified as a young teen when the story first hit the newspapers. As an adult, the pressure continued once again when the focus was placed on him with the release of the book and the film. He must have been so frightened that people would find out he was the possessed boy. Hopefully he avoided seeing the film and the horrific way it depicted his experience in such a graphic manner, but at the same time, I have to wonder if his curiosity drove him to the movie theater. This was one of the biggest movies of all time.

If you can, for just one moment, stop and remember what it was like to be a teenager and living with insecurity. Remember the changes within with your body, your emotions - how did it make you feel? Now take those feelings and place them on this fourteen-year-old boy who just lived through one of the most violent paranormal events in history. If you can do that for just one moment, you will look at this case and this boy in a whole new way. No, Roland Doe was not a monster at all. He was a typical fourteen-year-old boy who was reacting in the same way all fourteen-year-olds would react under the circumstances. He was still in many ways a child. You have to agree that the treatment of this boy was profane, horrible, and unjust. No matter your opinion of the case, Roland indeed was carelessly handled. The life he was forced to live after the case ended was completely unfair. Time cannot and will not erase those events for Roland Doe, no matter what he remembers. Popular culture has not let him forget. Society played its part in this diabolical game. Even I am somewhat guilty of not helping him to forget, and because of that, I can at least have the decency not to share his identity.

Roland's story has become part of pop culture history. Roland as well as those involved in the case have become religious icons in history. Whether you choose to invest your beliefs in the case, whether you believe the devil exists or is a fallacy, one fact remains; something happened to this boy - an event of such monumental proportions we are still discussing it today.

Father Bowdern

Father Malachi Martin writes in his book, *Hostage to the Devil*, "The recent vast publicity about Exorcism has highlighted the plight of the possessed as a fresh genre of horror film. The essence of evil is lost in the cinematographic effects. And the exorcist, who risks more than anyone else in an exorcism, flits across the screen as necessary but, in the end, not so interesting as the sound effects."

Father Martin talks about the price that an exorcist has to pay for their role in the exorcism; a price that a diabolical creditor will eventually come to collect.

The exorcist is the centerpiece of every exorcism. On him depends everything. He has nothing personal to gain. But in each exorcism he risks literally everything that he values ... Every exorcist must engage in a one-to-one confrontation, personal and bitter, with pure evil. Once engaged, the exorcism cannot be called off. There will and must always be a victor and a vanquished. And no matter what the outcome, the contact is in part fatal for the exorcist. He must consent to a dreadful and irreparable pillage of his deepest self. Something dies in him. Some part of his humanness will wither from such close contact with the opposite of all humanness - the essence of evil; and it is rarely if ever revitalized. No return will be made to him for his loss. (1992)

What price did Father Bowdern have to pay for his role in ridding Roland Doe of the devil? It has been reported that Father Bowdern lost a lot of weight from the fasting, which was required of him during the exorcism. In the article "Hell of a House" for the St. Louis *Riverfront Times*, Betty LaBarge, an eighty-year-old relative of Bowdern, shares that she had the priest over for dinner late into the exorcism, saying he must have lost thirty to forty pounds during it. "He looked terrible, just fatigued. When we asked him what was wrong, he simply turned the conversation. It wasn't until years later we learned he played the leading role in the exorcism. Still he never did talk about it. The word came from others involved" (Garrison). It was also reported by his brother, who was a physician, that Father Bowdern had puss-oozing boils on his body. We need to keep in mind the amount of physical abuse he endured during the violent episodes of the exorcism. As I reflect back to the last passages in Father Bishop's diary, the final days of the exorcism were particularly vigorous. Father Bishop pointed out that Father Bowdern would not stop praying next to the boy, day or night, no matter his weakened condition. He had to be dead on his feet, but his need to help this boy and to deliver him once again to God's grace was his driving force. I can visualize Father Bowdern at the bedside praying. I imagine him thin and frail from sustaining the horrific abuse. Neither defeated nor spiritually weak, he continues praying for the soul of Roland, ignoring his own strife. This picture is sad, moving, frightening, and stunning all at the same time.

It was reported that Father Bowdern had long lasting and debilitating effects from the exorcism, effects that were never publicized. Again, the focus being mainly on the boy, the fate of Father Bowdern was somehow lost in the shuffle of it all. In a 2013 article titled "Canonization for a Jesuit Exorcist?" Matt C. Abbot writes, "One Jesuit told me years ago that Father Bowdern had been seen stumbling down the hallway in the mornings prior to celebrating Mass. A Jesuit who witnessed this was understandably concerned, thinking it might have been alcohol-related. He went to his superior, who told him that Father Bowdern had been involved in an exorcism, and this 'stumbling' was an effect of having (successfully) performed the exorcism. After celebrating Mass, Father Bowdern was fine." If this report is true, then Father Martin's words of warning about the effects of exorcism on exorcists ring true. Indeed, a part of Father Bowdern was lost within those weeks with Roland Doe. Even more horrific is idea it might have impacted not only on him physically, but spiritually as well. That Father Bowdern was fine after celebrating mass questions whether the diabolic was somehow still attacking him even years and decades after the exorcism concluded. Father Bowdern lived a long life. He was eighty-six years old when he passed on April 25, 1983.

Father Martin writes that while Roland may remember nothing after the exorcism, this is not the case for exorcists. "They carry nagging doubts and bitter conflicts untellable to family, friend, superior, or therapist. Their personal traumas lie beyond the reach of soothing words and deeper than the sweep of any consoling thoughts" (1992). Father Bowdern carried his secrets with him to his grave. He would not work on the book or the film with William Peter Blatty because he refused to reveal the identity and the details of the exorcism of Roland Doe. What did Father Bowdern think of the film, *The Exorcist*? In the interview with *Spirit Daily*, Father Halloran explained, "I saw it right after it came out. I went with Father Bowdern and I thought it was a typical Hollywood, glitzy thing, real bizarre, trying to bring people to be fearful or to scream. I was disappointed with it. I thought it was a mess. And Father Bowdern did too. He gave sort of a running negative commentary throughout the whole movie. I thought the two of us were going to be thrown out of the theatre" (Brown).

Father Bishop

There is not much more written about Father Bishop other than he and Father Van Roo kept the details and identity of the boy anonymous because they believed it was their duty to keep it concealed. Father Bishop taught at St. Louis University until the 1950s when he was sent to Creighton University in Omaha, Nebraska. That is where he remained until his death. He was born January 15, 1906 and he died February 1978. His diary was never written for public consumption. This is evidenced by his insistence not to discuss the case. His tight-lipped approach is a confirmation to his honesty and integrity in the explanation of the events. However, I do not think he would be pleased that his diary was used over and over in the way it has been. In a way I feel guilty for sharing part of it with you. Still, Father Bishop lived during an era where possessions and hauntings were not casually discussed. I am not even sure if he ever understood the religious and historical significance of his diary. What Father Bishop shared with the world in his diary makes you question your faith and spirituality. It also brings forth the notion that if this can happen to someone like Roland Doe, it can happen to anyone.

The other aspect to consider with Father Bishop is that he not only kept a record of the case, but he was also the first of the exorcism team to come in contact with Roland. He worked as part of the exorcism team day in and day out. He witnessed the horrors and the final success of the exorcism. It is almost for certain that he carried his own demons with him from what he witnessed during those dark days in 1949. Fr. Malachi Martin completes this thought, "They share their punishment with none but God. Even that has its peculiar sting of difficulty. For it is a sharing by faith and not by face-to-face communication. But only thus do these men, seemingly ordinary and commonplace in their lives, persevere through the days of quiet horror and the nights of sleepless watching they spend for years after as their price of success, and as abiding reminders that, once upon a time, another human being was made whole, because they willingly incurred the direct displeasure of living hatred" (1992).

Father Halloran

Father Halloran was still a seminary student during the case. That is why within the diary he is referred to as Mr. Halloran. It is also important to keep in mind that he was not present for all of the events and by his admission was pulled off of the case five days before its conclusion. By all accounts, including his own, the last moment of his involvement with Roland Doe was the Holy Thursday before the final exorcism took place.

Father Halloran was also the only one involved in the exorcism to voluntarily share information with the public. He stopped short of identifying the boy, but he was the only one who would discuss the case. Most of his testimonies concerning the events of the exorcism match up, for the most part, with the diary. However, when asked if he thought the boy was possessed in an interview, he stated, "No, I can't go on record, I never made an absolute statement about the things because I didn't feel I was qualified" (Brown). That determination was not his call to make, and you have to respect the fact that he stuck with what I am sure he considered to be a chain of command. In 1966 Halloran volunteered for chaplain duty with the United States Army. In 1969, he volunteered for paratrooper training and then went to Vietnam. He would go on to say that he saw more evil in Vietnam than what he ever saw in the boy's hospital bed back in 1949 (Walker). In 2003, Halloran was diagnosed with cancer. He retired to the St. Camillus Jesuit Community in Wauwatosa, Wisconsin. He died on March 1, 2005. He was the

last of the surviving Jesuits who assisted in the 1949
Exorcism Case.

Chapter 19
Inspired

I first heard about the Roland Doe case like many other Americans did during the early-to-mid-seventies with the release of the book and film, *The Exorcist*. According to Box Office Mojo, if you figure in ticket inflation since 1973, *The Exorcist* earned over nine hundred million dollars since its original release. This film was a sociological phenomenon. People were vomiting and passing out in the aisles and lobbies of theaters. The public hysteria that surrounded the theatrical release had people standing in line for hours to experience the film. Theater owners had to hire security just to deal with the massive crowds that would line up outside of the theaters, some as early as 4:30 a.m. by some accounts. Interesting enough, it was said that more men were fainting in the theaters and lobbies than women. Those who were deeply disturbed by the film entered the theater with a predetermined belief that the devil existed, or they were devout Roman Catholics. It was quite a spectacle. One gentleman who passed out and broke his jaw on the seat in front of him sued Warner Brothers, settling out of court for an undisclosed amount.

The film's special effects horrified audiences. The character of the young girl, Regan, spoke vulgarities in a demonic tone, behavior quite shocking to a 1973 audience. Although Regan was twelve years old, her possessed state caused her to commit blasphemous acts of profanity and lewdness. Her head spun around 360 degrees and her throat swelled and pulsated. She vomited pea soup, levitated, and lay in a possessed state as her eyes rolled back into her head. Most shockingly of all, she masturbated with a crucifix while the demon spoke through her screaming, "Fuck me Jesus." That alone was enough to make people leave the theater, turn away from the screen, shake in their seats, and hide their eyes.

Why did this particular film strike such a deep chord with the 1973 audience? It is no secret that William Peter Blatty, a deep Roman Catholic, wrote the novel and film to bring a new, young audience to the Church. He believed it was an "apostolic work" that was brought about by divine intervention. You need to look at what was happening in the world and at home when the novel and the film were released to understand the nerve it was hitting with audiences. The demon was evil personified through the fears of a world that had seen genocide, the Kennedy assassination, the lies of Nixon, the atrocities of the Vietnam War, the growing generation gap, and of course the change of the family as well. In an article for *History Today*, Nick Cull took an analytical view of the novel and the film's impact on the society of the 1970s.

The action of The Exorcist takes place within a realm that had been uniquely privileged in American post- war culture: the home. The evil is doubly disturbing for erupting in so familiar a setting. The poster for the film traded on this. A man with a suitcase stands on a street, silhouetted in the light from a bedroom window over the caption:

'Something almost beyond comprehension is happening to a girl on this street, in this house, and a man has been sent for as a last resort. This man is The Exorcist.' The sacred sphere of the home is at risk. The family context is no less eloquent. Blatty's story clearly reflects contemporary fears over the breakdown of the family. Regan is the child of a 'broken marriage.' Her mother is caught up in her career and alternates neglect with cloying over-compensation. The early manifestations of the demon as an 'imaginary friend' seem like a substitute for the girl's absent father. A different sort of Father restores the situation. Beyond this The Exorcist plays on the guilt of women moving into the workplace and 'usurping the masculine role.' To this end, the mother is given a male name: Chris. The events that follow beg to be read as a punishment for nothing more than being a woman of her time. (2000)

Guilt is a serious thought and emotion on whatever level it is playing upon. It seems to me that Nick Cull had his finger right on society's pulse. The demon was already within all of us. The demon was our frustrations, our guilt, our desires, our anger, our addictions, our morals, and our fear of a world that was changing way too fast. Never before in history had people been through so many real-life horrors and changes in their lifetime. When you stop and really take a look at the world of the late 1960s and early 1970s, the hysteria surrounding *The Exorcist* becomes very clear.

I was only ten years old at the time of the release of the film, and of I course was not allowed to see it. My mother's response to the request was, "Absolutely not." It would be years later before I actually was able to see the film in its entirety thanks to VHS tapes. However, during the time of its theatrical release, it was impossible not to see pictures, film clips, articles, and even reports on events surrounding the film on the evening news. Warner Brothers expertly reported in its press kit that the film was based upon a true story. Of course people in St. Louis would talk about the film being based on a case that happened here at Alexian Brothers Hospital with a young boy. Thinking back now, one of the most frightening aspects of hearing the true story surrounding the film was the fact that it happened right here while I was growing up in St. Louis.

In September 7, 1993, an article called "Diary of an Exorcism" came out in the *St. Louis Post-Dispatch* written by John M. McGuire. I was an adult with children of my own. I read the article and found myself fascinated by the story once again. One person would say the exorcism was performed here and then you would hear another person say it was performed there. There seemed to be a lot of confusion about what happened and where it happened. I have heard so many stories throughout the years and seen so many broadcasts and films that made completely unsubstantiated claims. At this point in my life, I had absolutely no interest in the paranormal at all; as a matter of fact, I looked at this case from a strictly spiritual and religious perspective. That of course would change a number of years later when I stood face to face with a demon myself.

The article incited historical interest within me. This case is historical from whatever perspective you decide to view it from. Whenever I would come across an article or book on the true case, I would read it. I would watch any documentary or film dealing with it as well. It was more of a historical interest of trying to understand the significance of the events that occurred here in my home city while trying to solve the mystery. To my surprise, fellow St. Louisans were usually eager to talk about what they had heard and what they knew. It was a great time to gather tidbits of information from those who lived during the exorcism and those who lived with the aftereffects of the case. People wanted to talk about it. Most of this oral history has died off with the passing generation.

On May 18, 2001, my entire perspective on the case changed when I moved into a haunted house of my own, which the Roman Catholic Church deemed as a diabolical infestation, oppression, and possession in a 2012, 156-page report. My interest in the 1949 Exorcism Case switched from a historical interest into a personal one. I was looking for answers as to why things were happening to my family, and the only place to even try to gain an understanding at the time was to look at the cases in history that were like it; the 1949 Exorcism Case was part of this search for answers. I even turned to St. Louis University to see if they could direct me to some sort of help. Of course the answer at this time was no, and I got more than my share of the runaround, but it seemed to me that if they were able to help Roland Doe, they just might be willing to help my family. With the lack of help and the lack of cooperation, I was faced with figuring out how to help myself, driving me deeper into the research of the 1949 Exorcism Case. However, the further I jumped off of the research cliff, the more questions I found myself having.

One of the first major dilemmas of the case was figuring out the true locations. There are so many locations rumored to have been part of this case, it truly blows the mind. Out of the numerous St. Louis locations that were rumored to be part of the case, my research narrowed it down to five main locations. Four of these locations can be validated in Father Bishop's diary. The fifth is a location we will discuss in depth later - a location that has never been shared completely before this book. The four locations mentioned in the diary are the uncle's house, Alexian Brothers Hospital, St. Francis Xavier College Church, and the White House Jesuit Retreat. Any other locations in my well-researched understanding are either part of urban legend or part of a possible smoke screen in order to hide certain truths of the 1949 Exorcism.

Some might argue that where the furniture from the hospital room is stored should be considered part of these locations, but the truth is it is nothing more than a glorified storage facility, nothing more and nothing less. The real story lies within the five locations. Do I think it is important from a historical aspect that the furniture should be pre- served? Absolutely I do. I also don't think it's wise to let the furniture fall into the wrong or unknowing hands because of the possibility of residual negative energy. I believe it was a smart move by the Alexian Brothers to lock the room with everything in it after the exorcism, and I also believe it was wise to put the furniture out of the public reach. But after Father Bishop's diary was removed from the drawer during the 1978 demolition of that wing of the hospital, the furniture has become nothing more than historical artifacts.

Until September of 2005, most of the research I acquired was from reading. But that September I was approached by someone (who shall remain nameless for their protection) with unprecedented access to some of the locations involved with the case, including the mysterious fifth location. It was on this September night that my research was no longer literary - it turned into a paranormal investigation of the case. Up until this time, no other paranormal investigator had attempted to look into this case from an investigation point of view. There have been some investigators in the past who have tried to latch onto my research and my work on these locations and call it their own. However, they were not part of the research I conducted from 1993 forward, and they were not part of the first investigations I did on the case. These were people who I used to call friends - the people who have time and time again tried to take credit for the years of research I put into this case. The only reason I am stating it here now is an attempt to finally, once and for all, set the record straight on this issue. For the record, I have no problem with anyone wanting to investigate any of these locations. They are part of our religious and paranormal history. They should be revered and investigated by anyone who is brave enough to do so. However, for anyone who wants to take credit for the work and the years of research I have put into this case, I do, and will, have a serious problem with. I hope this settles this issue for the record.

The journey really begins here with new questions and a new understanding of the case. Research and analysis is just one aspect of investigation. The other part of the investigation should always be a physical, hands-on approach.

Chapter 20
Alexian Brothers Hospital

For years it has been rumored that the Alexian Brothers Hospital, now St. Alexius, is haunted because of the events that took place there in 1949. I have personally spoken with people who worked at the hospital recently and people who worked there prior to 1978. In 1978, the wing where the exorcism of Roland Doe took place on the fifth floor was demolished. All of these people have stories about personal occurrences that took place within the walls of the hospital. All of these people attribute these happenings to the 1949 Exorcism Case.

I recently found a blog written by KSDK St. Louis news anchor Pat McGonigle discussing a woman who personally called him after seeing a story he did on the priests who performed the exorcism.

Alexian Brothers Hospital

The woman who worked at Alexian Bros as a first-year nurse in the '70s claims she used to hear incredibly loud noises from a floor above her during her overnight shift. She said it sounded like homeless people fighting. She complained about it to coworkers and finally a security guard said to her, "Don't you know what happened on that floor? That's the exorcism floor." She didn't believe him, so the security guard took her up on that supposedly infamous floor. The entire floor was locked down and shuttered. Iron gates on either side of it, completely abandoned. He walked her down to the room where the exorcism happened. She said it was a floor for the criminally insane. Doors with heavy locks that opened out into the hallway with slots on the bottom to slide flood trays along on the floor. She says he showed her the room in question through a tiny window in the door. She said she can still see it today. A bed with a drop cloth over it. A desk with a cloth over it and a chair with cloth over it. On the wall, at the head of the bed, a huge black hole. She said the cop told her that's where the evil spirits exited the boy's body at the end of the exorcism. He told her they painted over it dozens of times, but the big black stain on the wall always came back. A few days later, she was filling little paper medicine cups on her floor. A process that took about an hour. She then walked down the hall and the lights flickered on and off. She kept walking down the hall, past these huge 12 foot statues of angels and saints they had in the old wing of Alexian Bros hospital. She claims she walked past one of the huge statues, looked up, and saw black eyes on one of the stone statues go from looking straight ahead, to looking at her, and then looking straight ahead again. She threw the tray in the air, ran to her nurse's station and quit on the spot.

This is not a unique story. Most of those who have had experiences describe events much like this. The interesting aspect of their stories is that they are all afraid to speak publicly about it. Some have stated they are afraid people will think they are crazy. There are some who fear some type of retribution for telling the things they know. Some have even gone as far as to suggest they felt it was part of an employee contract to never speak about these things publicly; however, I am sure that is just an excuse to avoid speaking publicly. No matter what the true reasons are, the truth remains - something is going on there, even if it might be a psychological impact of knowing the location's horrific past.

In the autumn of 2014, I met a woman who had been a nurse in the old Alexian Brothers Hospital. She did not want me to share her name, like many of the other professionals who worked in the building. Here is her testimony.

I was eighteen years old and began my nursing career as a nursing assistant at the Alexian Brothers Hospital. I had been there a few months on the night shift, which, at times, was not very busy. I had heard of the fifth floor and the rumors but never found any reason to go up to it. It was a slow night and one of the maintenance men had stopped by for coffee and a bit of talk. He asked if I had "seen it" yet. Said I had not and had no interest to. The conversation went on until going to the fifth floor became a dare. Having never been afraid to take a dare, and more to prove myself to them, I said, "Let's go."

We took the service elevator because all the other ones did not stop at the fifth floor. No one said anything as the doors opened, and the light from the car was the only brightness given to the floor. When they closed, it became very dark and the only light now was that of a small emergency light with two bulbs off to my left. But it was a large open area as I stood there and looked around. More open space than a normal nursing station would have had. Without leading me any further, I was only instructed to turn toward the right down the hallway. I started to walk to the right and observed several things immediately. The air was heavy and the smell of dust was everywhere. There was nothing on the wall, any wall. No pictures and no crucifix anywhere, which was odd being a Catholic hospital. Maybe it was just the darkness, but the hallway seemed to shrink down to only a four-foot walkway, very uncommon especially for a hospital. Walking became difficult only because there had been construction of some kind and the floor was littered with debris such as small pieces of plywood cut into odd shapes along with pieces and sections of two-by-four boards. No one followed me and I found that odd. There was no sound other than their direction to me in a low voice.

As I walked on, slowly due to all the debris and mess left, I saw an empty room on the right with no door. Even stranger was that the doorframe had been reconstructed with a new wooden frame. I looked around and noticed the whole hallway had been reconstructed. But none of it new. I remember the blackness as some of the wall seemed to be covered with what I thought might be thin tarpaper. But nothing seemed finished. Some of the framework had plywood covering it and some hadn't. I could hear those behind me softly telling me to keep going.

I went on until I reached the door the world seemed to fear. It was like nothing I had ever seen before. The door to the room was very solid and I could see no handle to it at all. Instead there was, in front of it, a steel bar door like those you would see in a jail or prison. But it was regular size, not large like a regular hospital room door. But the thing that stood out the most were the chains crossing the iron door. They were the large linked chains that some have called "log chains" in the logging industry. It was all bound together with a padlock, a very old fashioned lock I had only seen in movies. And it was all covered with a rusty dust. I just stood there for a minute no sure what to think or feel. The solid door, the barred door, and the chains were there and sealed tight, very tight, so that the very dim emergency lighting could never have been seen on the other side. I made my way back to the elevator a bit easier as my eyes had adjusted to the darkness. When the elevator door opened and light seemed to flood the area I looked around one more time. I had been told the fifth floor was now used for storage and there was no reason for me to be up here. But there was nothing anywhere you would find in a storage area. Only the cut pieces of wood and the dust was all there was. No one spoke until we reached my floor, and then it was only a "see you later" kind of thing. And that was about the end of that. I still don't know if I disappointed them by not running like a scared child or if I impressed them by not letting them see any fear in me.

Yet it was two weeks later I was instructed to take a body down to the morgue. It was an older hospital so after you open the door to the morgue you have to step in and reach for a pull string to turn on the light. It was very dark and I was having a great deal of trouble finding the light chain. This had never been a problem before. Then suddenly to my right I saw a black shadow, more of a mass, move three feet toward me. I regret to this day that the gurney, as well as the body, were pushed quickly into the room and the door closed as fast as I could! I'm not looking for a connection but I had never had any problems before.

I can't help but to believe that it was my strong fundamental Christian beliefs then as well as now that help keep me safe.

195

I find her description of the fifth floor and the way the door was locked very interesting. Numerous people have also reported that they were told there was no reason to go up there because it was only used for storage. Also interesting is the fact that it was one of the maintenance men who again incited the visit to the fifth floor. This seems to help corroborate the other nurse's story that was reported by McGonigle. There is another aspect of her eyewitness testimony that I found to be very interesting - you had to take a service elevator to get on the fifth floor. The use of a service elevator also comes into play in much the same way at another location will be discussing a little later within the case.

The old psychiatric wing of the hospital was demolished in October 1978 and with it the room Roland occupied on its fifth floor. Prior to this demolition, the room was unlocked and it is said that a worker went into the room and found Father Bishop's diary in a desk drawer. Now this is where the whole furniture thing gets a little foggy. It has been said the furniture was locked in a storage room in the basement. Supposedly, the brother who unlocked the storage room with the furniture would not enter the room. The furniture was then sealed in a wooden box and taken to be locked away and forgotten at Scott's Air Force Base in Illinois. Here is where the question is raised on this story. We have an eyewitness who says she had entered the room and others have said the exact thing, and the furniture was still in the room. The diary was found in a desk in the room on the fifth floor. Why would only some furniture be locked downstairs in the basement? And what of the eyewitnesses who say the furniture was in the room when it was opened for them on the fifth floor. So where was the furniture actually located in the building? Seems to me that the whole basement and the "afraid brother" story is part of the over-dramatization that happens continually with this case. I have no doubt the furniture was and still is kept in storage. However, this is a good example of how the legends start and how they flourish with dramatic effect.

There is also a story about the workmen opening the door to the room and something evil like a black cat or rat running from the room. However, this did not deter the men from entering the room. There were also reports that the wrecking ball would not hit the building until prayers had been spoken over it. Whether any of this is true or part of some very active imaginations will never be known, but the hype and impact this case had on the psyche of the residents of St. Louis make for some interesting stories surrounding this location and its history.

In September of 2005, I visited the site of the hospital, which is now St. Alexius, and very little of the original Alexian structure remains intact. The hospital is still a working hospital but looks very different from what was once located on the property. The chapel is still intact, which is the same chapel that was available to Roland and where he took part in Mass on that Tuesday morning fol-lowing his ordeal with the devil. You would think that by stepping into this location you would be instantly overwhelmed with a sense of evil or dread, when in fact, like most of the locations, there is a sense of spiritual peace within its walls. When I stepped up to the altar, I came to realize that the overwhelming sense of peace I felt radiated from the location itself. This is a place where prayers were said day and night for a young boy battling for the salvation of his soul. This is where masses were given on behalf of the boy. This is where Roland came once the exorcism was complete to solidify his faith and give thanks to God after his ordeal.

There is a positive vibe, which seems to emanate from its very foundation. A picture was taken from the back of the chapel looking down the center aisle past the pews. There was something interesting about the photo that was taken while I was there. On the right side of the aisle about halfway up there is a white misty figure that appears to be kneeling next to a pew. When I first looked at the photo many years ago, I could clearly see a nun kneeling to pray. Later when I looked at the photo I could see a demon-being low to the ground. When the photo has been shown to people without explanation, some people will see the nun and then others will see the demon. I think the interesting aspect of the photo is whatever way you want to view this case determines what you will see. If you prefer to see the glory of the battle, which was won at this location, you will see the nun. If you want to focus upon the possession and the negative horrors it brought down upon this boy, you will see the demon. I now see both the nun and the demon. I think that is because of my understanding wherever evil is present there is also grace. I think the photo, which was taken on that evening, illustrates it completely.

Shannon Lusk and I have visited this site on numerous occasions. We have visited the crack in the pavement of the parking lot that people claim can never be filled because it is in the exact spot where the exorcism happened five stories above. I have on several occasions facilitated ghost box sessions at this location with Shannon and with others. Like in all of the other locations, one message is always clear—a voice in each of the locations will say the number, "SIX." This is usually the first thing that will be said each and every time.

What is the significance of the number six? One of the most significant associations of the number is Jesus was accused of being demon-possessed six times in the Bible. Six also signifies the weakness in man; it also refers to the evils of Satan and the manifestations of sin. When you combine three sixes together, you have the mark of the beast in Revelation. Revelation 13:18, "Here is wisdom. Let him that hath understanding count the number of the beast: for it is the number of a man; and his number is six hundred three-score and six."

On one late Sunday afternoon I visited the hospital with my partner Rick Brandt. While attempting contact with the ghost box, we asked the question, "What did you think of the possessed boy?" The reply was quick and given in a very low and sinister tone, "We hated the damn boy." We both looked at each with shock upon our faces. Two nights later, Rick was sleeping and was woken when his little dog Rosie began to bark at something, which Rick could not see at the bedroom doorway. He could tell it was walking into the room by the way Rosie was backing up. She looked fixated on something as she barked viciously. All of sudden she yelped and ran into the bathroom adjacent into the bedroom, refusing to come out. Finally, Rick got her to settle down and checked everything and found absolutely no reason for her reaction, so he went back to bed. When he was laying there in the dark, he felt something begin to caress his face, over and over. Then, with a loud sound, it breathed into his face and was gone. I thought I would share this with you as a warning about these locations. Even though the exorcism was complete, you need to understand that residual negative energy can and does exist within these locations. So please by all means approach these locations, if you must. But be protected and aware of the possibility of this remaining negativity, which can follow you home.

Chapter 21
St. Francis Xavier College Church

In the early 1990s I worked for the Fox Theater in St. Louis Midtown, which is just about a half of a city block north from St. Francis Xavier College Church, on the edge of the St. Louis University campus. This was shortly before I started researching the Exorcism Case in 1993. The church itself is a beautiful white gothic stone structure with a steeple that soars high above in the sky. It is not dwarfed at all by the Continental Building, which stands close by.

It is a beautifully designed church that is not only a city landmark but is on the National Historic Registry as well. One night during my tenure in the midtown neighborhood, I had to take a city bus because of car problems. The bus stop was in front of the church at this time, and I remember I sat down on the front stairs of the church to wait for the Grand Bus to take me to my home on Flad. It was a beautiful autumn night that was clear and crisp. It was fairly late because we had been working on ticketing for the St. Louis premiere of *Phantom of the Opera*. I remembered sitting there enjoying a moment's peace. I leaned back to rest my arms on the stairs behind me and looked out across the midtown skyline toward downtown. I was lost not in thought, but at the pure peace when I heard someone say, "Hey," directly into my ear. I turned around, but there was no one there, and I kind of laughed, thinking to myself that my mind was playing tricks on me. I leaned back once more to take in the clear, cool night air when it happened again, "Hey." I sat up and looked behind me and saw no one there. I got up and walked down the steps to the sidewalk. I walked to the corner of the building, expecting to see a homeless person on the other side. I could see my bus pulling up the street, so I hurried to the bus stop to jump on. I jumped on the bus leaving the whole incident behind me. It was not until about a year later when I began researching the case that I found out the beautiful old church played a part in the case.

It's ironic that you can sometimes travel down a road without knowing its purpose and meaning all along. My experience with the church that night seemed like one of those moments. I call these the 20/20 moments - you know, after that old saying "hindsight is 20/20." While sitting outside of that church that night, I had no idea I was going to be taking the journey that would later involve the church and another building, which stood next to it in 1949.

The church rectory was where the boy was taken. There are no indications the boy was taken into the church. However, I have been told on more than one occasion that the basement of the church and the basement of the rectory were once connected. It was also mentioned that they would take Roland in through the side of the church into a recessed walkway. This walkway connected into a basement and the fathers would walk him through the basement of the church and into the basement of the rectory. I am unsure of the validity of the story, for I have not seen any proof. I do know on the occasions that when Shannon Lusk and I have visited the church, there never seemed to be any way the basement of the two buildings could have ever been connected. However, the idea did make sense for the priests to travel back and forth through the basements in order to avoid the rain, snow, and cold, which can all be part of a brutal St. Louis winter.

From indications in the diary, it would seem that Roland was only in the church for brief moments. Using the church might have been a way for them to conceal Roland during his fits of possession. The recessed walkway on the side would have helped to conceal the convulsing, spitting, and cussing boy. The actual rectory where the boy stayed was demolished in 1966 to make way for the building that now stands in its place today. There is a pattern developing with the demolition of the two sites where Roland had been. It makes you wonder if the activity in these locations was the reason they were demolished. The hospital and the rectory were both rumored to have mysterious incidents taking place during and after Roland's stay there. Even though there are several eyewitnesses that can attest to the rumors, it still remains speculation.

In all fairness, St. Louis University likes to point out that the boy was only at the rectory for a very short time. However, it is also essential to point out some of his most violent episodes happened traveling back and forth to the rectory and while staying in the room there. If you remember, his condition seemed to even escalate upon moving him to the rectory. You have to keep in mind someone possessed will have an aversion to holy and blessed items. As for the church and its rectory, they might as well have been housing the boy in one huge blessed crucifix. Everywhere Roland turned he would have been face to face with a blessed object or something sacred, even in the room he was given.

The inside of the church is a magnificent site to behold. The Stations of the Cross are illustrated with stained glass and the altar shoots upward toward a semi-dome ceiling. There is lustrous marble floor throughout, and the natural ambiance is uplifting. It really is a beautiful sight to behold. I had a friend who once told me she somehow got turned around in the church and ended up in the balcony in a room. "It was kind of creepy up there and when they found me there, they were very upset and told me that no one was to be up there and it was very dangerous. There was just simply no reason for this reaction. It was a room and nothing more," she said. I have looked up at the balcony before while standing on the ground floor. It is a solid structure made of stone and marble, and there is a beautiful stained glass window located up there. There is a hefty rail around the balcony, so it seems pretty stable. Still, this person is very adamant that she felt as if the church itself was hiding something up there. The overwhelmingly creepy feeling she experienced led her to believe this balcony was dangerous.

Shannon Lusk and I have been almost everywhere we could possibly go in the church, excluding the upstairs balcony. The church for the most part has a very purposeful and peaceful feeling inside. However, there were two places where we have both on separate occasions felt uneasy. The first of the two was the stairway that descended into the basement, and the second was a certain area of the basement itself. This area was located outside the chapel area in the basement. We have often wondered if they could have possibly taken the boy from the rectory to the chapel for the Blessed Sacrament, or something along those lines, but to say it was a definite event would be unfair because there is simply no way of knowing. However, it does seem important to note.

The outside of the church is the same. There are a few areas where you are sometimes overwhelmed with a feeling of being watched, a feeling of dread, or simply a feeling of complete uneasiness. These areas are mainly at the sides of the building, in particular the recessed walkway.

We would never attempt ghost box sessions in the church for obvious reasons of respect and decency. We have taken photos in the church and on the grounds, with nothing of significance showing in either of the two areas. However, the first time we turned the ghost box on in front of the church while still in the car, we immediately got the same creepy female voice saying, "Six."

My feeling is the building that replaced the old rectory would be the place to investigate. However, my fear of going to jail far outweighs my desire to investigate. I will tell you - the closer you step toward the building, the more energy spikes you get and the more active the ghost box becomes. What it tells me is there is more of a concentration of residual energy, possibly from an event in that area. Shannon and I asked the ghost box closer to the building, "Can you tell us about the possessed boy?" The response came back soft-spoken and male, "We prayed for the boy." Then we asked, "Can you tell us who the demon was who possessed the boy?" A voice shot back on the box deep and low, "The devil." Shannon and I looked at each other with that look of accomplishment on our faces. I do not think she was surprised by the answer at all. I myself felt chilled at the response. The way it said "the devil" reminded me of the usage of "legion."

One of my favorite explanations of the night of the exorcism is told by *Spirit Daily.*

Easter Monday - as the priest prayed for the angel's intervention - as prayer intensified, with near desperation the boy's voice suddenly changed into a clear, commanding, and dignified voice from heaven. "Satan, I am St. Michael," said the voice that now came from the boy, "and I command you Satan to the leave the body in the name of Dominus (the Lord). Now. Now. Now!" At that precise moment what sounded like a loud gunshot was heard throughout the hospital. The boy sat up, had a vision of the archangel, and announced with near befuddlement but certainly terrific relief that the evil force was gone At the same time, priests at St. Francis Xavier Church saw a light illuminate the sanctuary from the dome high over the altar and in the light a vision of Michael. (Brown)

Father Halloran speaks about this moment in his interview with Michael Brown, "I understand there was a very loud sound, a boom - sort of like a sonic boom - and then the boy opened his eyes and said St. Michael came and that it was over. At the same time this took place there were about six or seven priests over in the college church saying their office and there was a huge boom over there and the whole church was completely lit up" (Brown).

I have to wonder why more attention is not placed on this miraculous moment that occurred at both locations. We are talking about eyewitness testimony to the appearance of the Archangel Michael and the supernatural event that triggered his appearance. Both of these places, the church and the hospital, should be considered holy places because of the event that took place in two locations on that Easter Monday in 1949. It clearly surpasses any other events of the possession. People gawk and visit these places in search of the devil, when clearly the attention has been misplaced on the devil instead of the appearance of Saint Michael himself. Clearly it was a significant religious and historical event, and it not only furthers the idea that these places should have held a special place within the religious community, but it also should further the call for canonization of Father Bowdern, who was the acting exorcist during the miraculous event.

Chapter 22
The White House Jesuit Retreat

The White House Jesuit Retreat is one of the most beautiful religious properties in St. Louis and the Midwest, if not the nation. It sits on the bluffs overlooking a spectacular view of the Mississippi River. I first visited the retreat back in 2007 during a beautiful autumn afternoon. I felt drawn to it for peace and serenity. It was during a difficult time when I needed those who once claimed to be friends, but I quickly found out they would rather walk away instead of being there for me the way I had been for them time and time again. I felt incredibly alone and discouraged at the moment, and God was the likely choice to turn to in an attempt to strengthen my faith. I have always found that in the most difficult moments in life, turning to my faith would allow me to feel better. Somewhere in my faith in God, I would find the answers I needed. That was exactly my hope on this day in 2007.

I need to point out that the retreat is not a place for sightseeing. It is a serious place for reflection upon faith. I called ahead and asked if I could spend the afternoon because I did not have time for a full retreat, and I was not refused. It should be noted I was given permission to be there.

Of course I had already heard the story of the harrowing afternoon Father Halloran had spent here with Roland those many years ago. In my mind, I have always felt that whatever gave Father Halloran the strength to save Roland on that day was some type of divine or angelic intervention. In my mind, it was also a place of some type of miracle; although, not on the scale of the appearance of Saint Michael during the final moment of the exorcism, but it still seems to me to be a moment of miraculous intervention.

This was the moment in the possession case where they could have easily lost the battle for Roland. It came incredibly close to happening. As I stood reflecting upon the crucifixion, I began to wonder, if the devil could orchestrate a failed attempt here, he could do it anywhere. But then I reminded myself it was indeed a failed attempt because by some unforeseen reason, Father Halloran was able to intervene. He made that tackle which saved the boy's life. I drew upon what remnants of positivity must still remain in that spot and soon I began to feel calm and peaceful once again. I left the serenity and beauty behind me and headed home.

When you stop and look at the first three of the locations we have just covered, you will see a theme present in each of them. In all three locations, the presence of the power of positive influence was at work, not only on the events but the people and locations themselves. There was a case I worked some years ago that ended in exorcism. I worked with two very spiritual and faithful men. One of these two was a Baptist preacher, and he said something at one point in the investigation that has stuck with me ever since, "If Jesus were to knock on your door right now to enter your house, would you be hesitant or even embarrassed to let him enter?" Obviously, the first three locations would clearly have been made available to Jesus. The power of devotion is found throughout each location and in the people residing within them.

In the Alexian Brothers Hospital, you have the brothers who were praying for the boy's deliverance from the grasp of possession. At St. Francis Xaviers College Church, the same type of behavior occurred night and day. The White House Jesuit Retreat was also a place of prayer and peace. The theme that is apparent in these three places is the devotion of the people and their faith to starve off the devil's attack. It makes me think of a preacher's words and the lesson I learned through my own trials, which is that "Evil cannot thrive within the face of positivity and devotion."

People ask me all of the time, "How do I keep myself safe from anything demonic?" The answer is easy. Get rid of the negativity in your life. Be devoted to your God and your faith, whatever it may be. Live your life with love and devotion toward others. Finally, learn to laugh because the devil hates a sense of humor. Wake up each morning and ask yourself this one question, "What am I thankful for?" Since we are discussing this point through a religious and spiritual viewpoint, what does the Bible say about living this type of positive existence?

Philippians 4:8 "Finally, brothers, whatever is true, whatever is honorable, whatever is just, whatever is pure, whatever is lovely, whatever is commendable, if there is any excellence, if there is anything worthy of praise, think about these things."

Proverbs 17:22 "A joyful heart is good medicine, but a crushed spirit dries up the bones."

Jeremiah 29:11 "For I know the plans I have for you, declares the Lord, plans for welfare and not for evil, to give you a future and a hope."

Ephesians 4:31–32 "Let all bitterness and wrath and anger and clamor and slander be put away from you, along with all malice. Be kind to one another, tenderhearted, forgiving one another, as God in Christ forgave you."

Romans 12:2 "Do not be conformed to this world, but be transformed by the renewal of your mind, that by testing you may discern what is the will of God, what is good and acceptable and perfect."

John 14:27 "Peace I leave with you; my peace I give to you. Not as the world gives do I give to you. Let not your hearts be troubled, neither let them be afraid."

1 Peter 3:9 "Do not repay evil for evil or reviling for reviling, but on the contrary, bless, for to this you were called, that you may obtain a blessing."

Romans 12:12 "Rejoice in hope, be patient in tribulation, be constant in prayer."

It is that easy. Devotion, love, faith, positivity, and humor are the things that made these places and the people in them able to thrive and work against the evil in the boy. I know what some of you must be thinking at the moment. Well, Steven, that is from a Christian point of view, and I am not a Christian. It does not matter what religion you are or if you even follow a religion or other spiritual beliefs. These are universal ideals to live by. I think we focus too often on our differences instead of embracing the ideas and things that work in our lives and make us human. For one moment, let's say the boy was not possessed by a demon or devil at all. Let's for one moment say he was possessed by ideas within himself. Even if he was not possessed by a demon, or consumed by his own fears, the medicine would still be the same. Be devoted to someone or something. Love as many people in this life that you can and hopefully you will be loved back in return. Have faith in something, even if that something is just getting up tomorrow morning or embracing the ability within yourself to survive. Be positive with whatever you can. I will tell you there was a time in my life when the only thing I could be positive about was the fact that I had not died in my sleep. From there I added more and more things, and the positive things began to pour into my life. Learn to laugh, even if that laughter involves finding humor in the hole you have currently dug for yourself. These are not religious ideals. These ideals are universal and can work within anyone's lives. They worked for people within these three locations and because of that, Roland Doe was saved, whether you want to believe in supernatural means or natural causes.

Chapter 23
The Uncle's House

I am going to state my feelings concerning this house right out of the gate. There is too much attention placed on it and the negative things that happened inside its walls. Too much of the negativity in this house is blamed on the demonic that resided in the boy in 1949, and in return it keeps feeding negativity back into the house. If there is or ever was diabolical activity left within this home, it was not from the 1949 Exorcism Case. This house has had more blessings and prayers of exorcism said in it than any house in this country. The misconception here is a house will automatically stay cleansed. There is a change in those living within the walls of the location that has to take place. Roland's family was a family who were dabbling in spiritualism not for enlightenment but greed. If that attitude did not change once the exorcism was complete, then something new could have entered. Of course it is possible for some negative residual energy to remain present. However, that energy would remain powerless and nonexistent if it isn't continually fed. Feed this house negativity and you will get what you ask for in return.

Many times paranormal locations, such as the exorcism house, are exploited financially for entertainment and paranormal teams seeking attention. For example, when a recent paranormal show entered the house, one of the main components of their investigation was to contact the supposed demon that infested Roland Doe. One of the consultants to this team claimed they had never been back in the house after filming the documentary because they were too afraid. However, after researching the consultant's background, photos and advertisements were found of this investigator holding $100 per person events after filming the documentary. There were also photos uncovered of this consultant standing in the living room of this house smiling and seemingly content during these events. During this show, the consultant provided the stars with an Ouija board to use in the bedroom where the boy slept. This consultant later claims they were adversely affected by the demon in the house. This was the demon of greed and had nothing more in common with the case than that. Any current activity that may be occurring in the house is very likely to have been caused by the parade of people and paranormal investigators who, with their film crews, have been to this house over and over again. However, it is to be noted the current occupants, who are in fact Atheists, have reported to the media that they have lived there since 2005 and have experienced nothing.

It is imperative to remember the demon enters through a point of origination. For the house or land in Cottage City, it would have been the planchette from the original board. For the uncle's house in St. Louis, the point of origination would have been the boy himself who became the oracle when possessed. Once the exorcism was complete, that would have cleared the St. Louis house, unless the behavior in that home was continuous, which would infect it once again. I find that very unlikely because of the ordeal Roland's uncle and family had experienced. What happened in the house after they left in the early 1950s is something that will remain an unknown factor. However, if paranormal investigators continue to play around with things they shouldn't, the activity will once again surge. If the house has a current diabolical presence in it, it was infected by them and not the 1949 case at all.

Chad Garrison, writer of the *Riverfront Times*, quotes one of the previous owners of the uncle's house in St. Louis who lived there from 1991 to 1999. The owner said he only learned of the home's occult past after purchasing it. He says it came as a shock, but maintained that nothing out of the ordinary ever occurred in the house while he lived there. "We loved that house...Way I see it, the place was blessed so many times during the exorcism, it's probably the safest home in all St. Louis" (Garrison).

However, we do know that there were others who lived in the house who claimed the bedroom where the boy slept was unusually cold and drafty. A neighbor and his wife who toured the house claimed that his wife became violently ill and had to rush from the house. One of the later residents will not even discuss what happened to them while living in the house. Another account speaks of a man who lived in the house for a short time but moved and was never heard from again. It is also fair and important to point out this is not an unusual occurrence for a haunted house to react differently with different people. The question would be, at this point, what within a person triggers this sort of activity? In the case of my house, it never had an exorcism performed in it or even a decent, proper blessing. There is a huge difference between an untouched haunted location and one that has been prayed for and blessed by an entire exorcism team - over and over again. At least it would seem that way. With this case, however, the mystery continues to build. Whatever the case, whether the house goes dormant for a period of time or something was brought into at a later date, the question remains, "Which came first, the demon or the egg?"

Shannon Lusk and I have been to the house on numerous occasions. I have to admit, once you pull up to the house, your eye is immediately drawn to the room Roland once occupied during the woes of his possession. There is an uneasy aura about the place, and you have to stop yourself from letting your imagination run wild. Even with my criticism of the paranormal shows that need to overdramatize in order to obtain ratings, I have to wonder exactly how much negative energy still lies within its walls. My problem is not with the shows at all but with those who like to add to the myth while clouding the truth. Regardless of my obvious criticisms of the charlatans who have tried to build careers around it and cash out on its obvious public appeal, I still believe it is a location that is an important part of our religious and supernatural history. It should be researched when available. The only way we are ever going to be able to drop the smoke screen surrounding the house is for honest and earnest research to be done in it.

There seems to be a theme of greed in this case. It started with the family's probing of the demons - questioning them about the whereabouts of the aunt's supposed fortune. The greed has continued to prosper with the obvious fleecing of the public with lies and delusions. It is also important to point out that if the demonic were still residing in this home, it would be very unlikely anyone would be able to live in it. However, there is a huge dichotomy between the first three locations and this house. Again, the majority of the attention regarding this case should have been placed on the devotion of the clergy, the salvation brought to Roland, and the dedication the Church had to this particular case.

It was the culmination of a battle where good defeated evil. Instead, we as a society are more interested in glorifying the parlor tricks of the devil and his minions. If we are going to go looking for demons, we will find them every single time. I can prove this to you over and over again in a world that is full of diabolic acts and evil. However, when we have the opportunity to observe the power of something enormously positive, we pass it by for the latter, which I will always find illogical and of course offensive.

Chapter 24
The Secret Revealed

F. Scott Fitzgerald wrote the following words in his novel *The Great Gatsby*, "This is a valley of ashes - a fantastic farm where ashes grow like wheat into ridges and hills and grotesque gardens; where ashes take the forms of houses and chimneys and rising smoke and, finally, with a transcendent effort, of men who move dimly and already crumbling through the powdery air. Occasionally a line of gray cars crawls along an invisible track, gives out a ghastly creak, and comes to rest, and immediately the ash-gray men swarm up with leaden spades and stir up an impenetrable cloud, which screens their obscure operations from your sight" (1925).

What Fitzgerald describes is much more than just a description of the Valley of Ashes. He is discussing the stirring up of smoke screens, or in this case, a screen of ashes to hide the ugliness of what lies beneath - hiding what might make some uncomfortable if they knew what was really taking place beneath the cloud of ashes. There are many reasons for truths to be hidden from the people. A lot of times you will hear our government claim it is for reasons of national security. As if we actually believe everything our government is hiding from us would put our nation at risk. Many times truths are hidden from society by those who feel that society is too fragile to handle the truth, so they are therefore left in the proverbial dark.

Remember that great line Jack Nicholson's character spoke on the witness stand in *A Few Good Men*, "You can't handle the truth! Either way, I don't give a damn what you think you're entitled to!" In the very same vein, I believe this is why the Church has hidden the truth about the 1949 Exorcism Case - by setting smokescreens, false locations, and stories into play in order to hide what it doesn't want you to know and doesn't feel you should know.

There is a clear reason, in my opinion, why those involved in this case kept the details concealed and took those secrets with them to the grave. I also believe there is a reason Roland and his parents never spoke publicly about the experience. I do not for one moment believe Roland could not and does not remember anything from his ordeal. I have worked a number of these cases and there is aware- ness in each and every one of them. I am not going to call out anyone in particular because I believe those involved felt they were doing the right thing not only for the Church but also for the people they served. It is also hard to tell who was actually in the know and knew the full extent and impact of the locations and the events being hidden from the public. I am not even sure I have a full understanding of the impact and implications of what I am going to share with you. I am sure it is going to be denied, redirected, and recounted time and time again from the moment this is published. It might simply be ignored, because without acknowledgment, it makes deniability much easier. Either way, there are a number of ways to look at it, and there are many different angles and theories that can be gathered from the knowledge of what I am calling the "Hidden Priest."

I think it is important to lay down a foundation of understanding before I reveal to you what I've experienced and come to understand as the truth about this case. In "Chief Exorcist Says Devil Is In Vatican," Nick Squires quotes Father Gabriele Amorth saying, "The devil resides in the Vatican and you can see the consequences ... He can remain hidden, or speak in different languages, or even appear to be sympathetic. At times he makes fun of me. But I'm a man who is happy in his work" (2010). Father Amorth, the eighty-five-year-old who has been the Holy See's chief exorcist for twenty-five years, addressed the "resistance and mistrust" toward exorcism among some Catholics, saying "His Holiness [Pope Benedict XVI] believes wholeheartedly in the practice of exorcism. He has encouraged and praised our work." Why would Squires choose the words "resistance and mistrust" when referring to some of those in the Church and their views on exorcism? Why would the Church resist or mistrust what they believe to be the work of God and part of the doctrine of spiritual warfare, which they preach? This statement alone coming from the Vatican raises a tremendous litany of questions.

It has been reported that Satan has resided within the walls of the Vatican since 1963. This is further evidenced by Father Malachi Martin in *The Keys of This Blood,* where he made reference to a diabolic rite held in Rome in 1963. "Indeed, [Pope John II] Paul had alluded somberly to 'the smoke of Satan, which has entered the Sanctuary'...an oblique reference to an enthronement ceremony by Satanists in the Vatican. Besides, the incidence of satanic pedophilia - rites and practices - was already documented among certain bishops and priests as widely dispersed as Turin, in Italy, and South Carolina, in the United States. The cultic acts of satanic pedophilia are considered by professionals to be the culmination of the Fallen Archangel's rites." Could there be factions in the Vatican and the Church itself that are trying to not only devalue the importance of the Rites of Exorcism but abolish it altogether? Not for the reason they might claim— because it is old world and archaic—but could they really believe in Satan, with factions within the Church worshiping him?

Remember the greatest trick the devil can play on society is to make people think he does not exist. This theme has risen more than once throughout this book referring to society's satanic denial and now has appeared once again in direct reference to the Church and its doctrines. There have been some who have reported that Vatican II was and is actually the work of the devil himself. "The evil influence of Satan was evident in the highest ranks of the Catholic hierarchy, with 'cardinals who do not believe in Jesus and bishops who are linked to the demon,'" according to Amorth (Squires). This is a strong statement coming from someone inside the walls of the Church.

In "Satanism in the Vatican," Archbishop Milingo is quoted saying, "The devil in the Catholic Church is so protected now that he is like an animal protected by the government; put on a game preserve that outlaws anyone, especially hunters, from trying to capture or kill it." Could the knowledge I am about to share with you have been part of a driving force within this faction of lies and deceit? There is a strong possibility that there are those in the Church whose sole purpose is to protect the devil. This could also explain a few things concerning this case and others we have discussed. Is this why the emphasis has not been placed on the two locations where Saint Michael appeared in the 1949 Exorcism Case? Could it also be why Father Bowdern has never been considered for canonization? Could it be why the Catholic Church has refused to label the case of Anneliese Michel as a true possession, refusing to consider her a candidate for sainthood?

Here is the point to understand before we get into the revelation of the secret. The Church is quite able to turn its head the other way when it feels the need to hide behind its walls; even more frightening is the factions in the confines of the Church who proclaim Christianity but serve the fallen. Interesting enough, this is not the first time I have come in contact with a possibility that some are trying to hide behind the guise of Catholicism in order to conceal a darker allegiance to the fallen. We have seen those in the Church's highest offices state that Satan has been present within the Church since the year 1963. In fact, Father Amorth could even be hinting at what I am about to reveal when the *Telegraph's* article continues, "In a rare insight into the world of exorcism, the Italian priest told *La Republica* newspaper that the 1973 film *The Exorcist* gave a 'substantially exact' impression of what it was like to be possessed by the Devil." With all of this in mind, it is time to reveal the secret behind the 1949 Exorcism Case.

In September of 2005, I was asked by a source that will remain unnamed - and will be referred to as only Person X - if I wanted to tour some of the St. Louis exorcism locations. Helen, who was also living through the Screaming House Haunting, was asked to go along as well. We have already discussed the hospital chapel we visited together on that night in 2005. However, there was one other location I was taken to.

Person X told me, "There is one other location which not too many people know even exists. Would you like to go there?" We had already visited what was once Alexian Brothers Hospital, and we had also visited St. Francis Xavier College Church on that same night. Of course my answer was, without a doubt, yes. It was only a short drive to this other location, which I cannot and will not for obvious reasons disclose exactly. We were taken to what appeared to be another hospital of some sort, with an elevated glass walkway that connected two buildings.

This hospital seemed substantially more deserted than even the small hospital that was once the Alexian Brothers Hospital. We entered one of the buildings through a pair of double doors where we were met immediately by a security guard standing next to a walk-through metal detector. He said hello and simply motioned us into the building as if he were expecting our arrival. There was no question or reference to what we were doing there. He just simply greeted us and motioned us through.

Person X told us we would be going upstairs to another floor. As we were ushered around a hallway on the bottom floor, the building appeared like any other medical facility. I can remember seeing beautiful, large white statues that seemed to be placed strategically throughout the downstairs lobby areas. We turned a corner and walked past a regular looking bank of elevators, which, to my surprise, we did not stop to use. Instead, we continued walking down a hallway when Person X stopped and used a key to open what appeared to be a regular door, but to our surprise, behind it was a small elevator with a dark, olive-green metal door.

We entered the elevator, pressing the number 4 on the keypad. The elevator was small and the three of us stood very close together within its confines. The elevator slowly rose to the fourth floor then gave that small slow drop in the way old elevators do when stopping. The olive-green metal doors opened and we stepped out into what appeared to be a hallway.

The hallway was long and was lighted with overhead lighting. It was not an unpleasant looking place at all. The walls were painted a baby blue and there was a white rail on the wall that ran the length of the hallway. There was also a dayroom on the left side of the hallway that spanned its entire length. The windows to the dayroom were reinforced with wire between panes of glass. As we began to walk down the hall, Person X said, "I want you to let me know if you get any feelings here or have any perceptions about this place." This really was not stated as a request and was stated without any type of emotion. I looked at Helen and she gave me a puzzled look. It was a strange request because neither of us had ever claimed to be psychic or anything of that nature. It also felt to me, and Helen would later agree, as if these locations were being tested on us for some type of reason. However, we continued our slow walk down the hall. At the very end of the hallway we could see two large double doors with two small rectangular windows in each, but each of these windows had been covered.

Walking down the hall past the dayroom windows, I could hear a noise as if someone was tapping on the glass on the other side. I stopped for a moment, thinking it might have just been the vibration from our walking, but there was no noise after stopping - nothing but silence.

At this moment, I walked up to the dayroom window and put my hand on it, and something from the other side of the window tapped on my palm. I pulled my hand away quickly. There was no one there. Person X asked me what had happened, and I told them. They gave no response, other than a shake of the head in acknowledgement as if they understood, and then we continued our journey down the hall toward the brown wooden double doors.

About halfway down the hall there was a deserted desk station in which a calendar from 1983 hung on the wall. A few pencils and pens were strewn haphazardly upon the desk. Person X looked at us and asked, "Do you know where you are?" I looked at the person with a puzzled look and both Helen and I shook our heads. "There was only one patient kept on this floor until 1983. It was a priest."

All of a sudden it hit me and I knew exactly where I was. I had heard rumors for years about this exact place. It was always told in the rumors that there was a priest who worked on the exorcism who was being kept in a mental ward in some hospital in St. Louis. All of a sudden the wires in the dayroom windows, the hidden elevator, and the covered windows on the door made complete sense to me. I knew where I was, and for a brief moment, a feeling of fear came over me, and then I have to admit that excitement quickly replaced it. I understood we were standing where very few people had been allowed. I also understood the implications of this place and what it meant to the Exorcism Case. William Peter Blatty, like Father Amorth stated, had gotten the story completely correct in his novel and film.

Person X continued, "This priest was kept here until his death in 1983. On his deathbed he grabbed his nurse by the throat and he said, 'I am going to kill you fucking bitch!' And then he died, collapsing back onto his bed." There was no emotion when Person X spoke about these events, which has always struck me as being odd. When I speak of it, even to this day, it is very hard to shut out the feelings of shock at the priest's last words before death. Person X continued, "Upon his death this floor was then deserted. The only ones who come up here now are the Church, which performs different types of paranormal experiments, and of course maintenance. It has stayed exactly the way it was on the day of the priest's death in 1983."

I began to move down the hall, this time a little farther ahead of Helen and Person X with longer strides than both of them, which was easy due to my excitement and my six-foot-seven frame. I reached the brown double doors at the end of the hall fairly quickly. I put my hand out to open one of the brown double doors. "Stop. You do not want to go in there. On the other side of that door is the actual room where the priest was kept."

Person X then instructed me to put my ear to the door, "Take a listen and you will see why." I did as I was instructed, and I could hear what sounded like things moving around and being thrown on the other side of the door. Things were moving around violently on the other side of the door, and as I listened, a cold chill ran through my entire body. All of a sudden, with a powerful blow, there was a *BOOM* on the other side of the door. Both doors swayed slightly outward with the concussion below my head. I jumped back from the double wooden doors in shock, my heart thumping out of my chest. Person X said, "See, I told you that you did not want to go in there." A slight smile was on their face, and it struck me that it was the first and only time I had ever seen Person X smile in any way.

Person X was completely right. I did not want to go in there because I knew exactly where I was standing. A feeling of dread of some sort came over me all of a sudden. Some- thing was telling me that Helen and I were in some type of danger, and the whole story as to why we were there was not being shared with us. I cannot explain it, other than to tell you the fight-or-flight instinct was beginning to kick in, and I wanted to go home because something in my gut was telling me there was something to seriously fear.

"Do you know where you are?" Person X asked without emotion once again. I said that I did and that I had heard about this place in rumors that were spoken about from time to time from many different people. Person X shook their head in agreement, and with that acknowledgment, we headed to the door and left for home.

There are times still when I stop and wonder what the purpose of taking us to this location and showing us these things was. I also have to wonder if that is why our own personal demonic case went completely out of control so quickly after the night of our visit to the mysterious floor. I have lived with this knowledge since 2005, and it has always bothered me. Now that Helen is no longer living and I am the only one left, I thought it would be wise to put down what I know so it can be remembered. I can only tell you the facts as they were shared with us, and I can only share my personal experiences from that night with you.

The final telling of what happened during the last moments of the exorcism in 1949 is still in question, and with this new knowledge we can only speculate. It appears to be very likely that the demon went into one of the priests that was present in the room during the final moments of the exorcism. I do not know or even wish to speculate which priest it was or even if that priest is named in the diary. My gut tells me that it is a different priest altogether, a priest that has never been mentioned and has never been associated with the case. It is clear to me with all of the evidence available, and with all of the remaining questions that have lingered through the years, that something else is and was being hidden. The numerous tellings of the events never seem to completely match up. The boy came in contact with somewhere around forty-eight different suspects who could have been the possessed priest in the hospital.

Blatty was not wrong when he wrote the ending of the novel and the film, depicting the demon going into Father Damien Karras in the last moments. In actuality, it appears that this is the way it happened, and instead of the possessed priest dying from a fall down a long flight of stairs, he was institutionalized for the remainder of his life. The horror of his circumstance and his existence were reduced to no more than whispers and rumors. I do find it interesting that Blatty's follow-up to *The Exorcist* includes Damien Karras inside an institution possessed by the Gemini Killer. There is no way to know if Blatty knew of the truth or had just heard the same rumors. However, there is a striking correlation between his telling and the events I have just shared with you. The first eyewitness report I heard of this possessed priest was from a patient who was kept on the other side of the same floor. The year of this patient's stay on the floor was sometime during the 1970s. I heard about this eyewitness testimony several years before my visit to the floor the priest was kept. During our visit, however, the entire floor had been deserted.

This is the secret I believe the priests took with them to their graves. I believe Father Halloran, who was not present for what he says were five days before that final night of the exorcism, and also admittedly was not present on that final night, might not have even known about this truth. Father Halloran was "taken off" the case, which brings up the question of whether they were systematically limiting outside exposure to the demon because they knew they were going to attempt a transference of sorts. It also brings up the question: did the possessed priest volunteer for the role he was about to play in the case, or did it happen by complete accident?

However, there are some inconsistencies in Father Halloran's interviews about those last moments of the exorcism. For example, even in the interview with *Spirit Daily* Father Halloran states, "I was taken off five days before the conclusion, but from what I understand there was a very loud sound, a boom - sort of like a sonic boom - and then the boy opened his eyes and said St. Michael came and that it was over. At the same time this took place there were about six or seven priests over in the college church saying their office and there was a huge boom over there and the whole church was completely lit up. Father Bowdern, who was doing the exorcism, and the boy were at the rectory" (Brown). I have always found this confusing because it has always been reported the final moments of the exorcism took place on the fifth-floor hospital room at Alexian Brothers. It also amazes me how no one else has ever really questioned this discrepancy while Father Halloran was still alive.

Another thing that I have to question is why the Church was performing different sorts of paranormal experiments on the mysterious deserted hospital floor since at least 1983, if not before the death of the reported possessed priest. It does make you question Father Amorth's revelation in which he states, "The 1973 film *The Exorcist* gave a 'substantially exact' impression of what it was like to be possessed by the Devil." He surely could not have meant the theatrics of the pea soup and head spins. Was he privy to the full knowledge of what I feel is the truth behind the case? Also important to remember is the claim from Roland who to this day remembers nothing, which when you keep other possessions in mind, is hard to fathom. It just does not follow through when others *do* remember at least parts of their time under possession.

Then there is the case of Father Malachi Martin, who some believed could have been cursed or murdered. According to an unnamed source, Father Martin stated that the fall that ultimately led to his death was the result of a push from an unseen force. "According to Fr. Charles Fiore, Martin's last book, *Primacy*: *How the Institution of the Catholic Church became a creature of the New World Order*, (the so called 'survival manual') was never completed. In fact, Fr. Fiore claimed he was in the process of editing the book himself at the time of Malachi's death. Questions remain as to whether the book was completed and somehow kept from circulation" (Henrie).

Another frightening aspect of sharing any of this with you is that there are those, including Father Martin, who feel there was and is a clear danger in revealing the Luciferian factions within the Church. "Fr. Malachi Martin was given tribute along with Fr. Fiore and Fr. Kunz on the website of *Roman Catholic Faithful* owned by Steven Brady. Brady was investigating cases of pedophilia by clerics and sought to alert the Catholic populace to the gravity of the problem. Frs. Kunz, Martin, and Fiore assisted and supported Mr. Brady in his efforts. Fr. Kunz paid the highest price: ritual murder" (Henrie). The article goes on to state, "The oaths of many secret societies include throat slicing as a penalty for revealing a group's closest secrets. Had Kunz exposed the operations of a cult? Kunz's friend and associate Malachi Martin certainly thought so. Six weeks after Kunz's murder, Martin appeared on a radio show claiming to have inside information that Kunz's murder was carried out by Luciferians. Luciferians are not your garden-variety devil worshippers, but they are devil worshippers nonetheless."

It also has been stated time and time again that between 1 to 5 percent of those who work within the Church practice worship of the fallen Archangel Lucifer. It is also said that many of those involved hold very high offices in the Church. Some believe the end of time is near and the Anti-Christ will actually make his appearance as a pope. The Church still believes in prophecy, and it appears that a lot of what is happening in the Church today has been prophesized many times throughout religious history, and some even feel it has been in the book of Revelation itself.

With everything considered, it is not too far a stretch of the imagination to believe a priest was allowed to become possessed in order to research, study, and communicate with the devil. Remember Person X telling us the Church had been performing different types of paranormal experiments in that deserted mental ward? What were those experiments and why were they being performed by the same religious body that warns against them? There is a real possibility that this all connects to what is happening in the Church today. The timing of everything we have spoken about here is not only uncanny, but the implications are frightening.

There are many more questions surrounding this possessed priest than there will ever be answers. However, I do feel it is important we look for a deeper understanding and truth where it is concerned. Was this deserted mental ward and the possessed priest it once housed part of Satan's game preserve that Archbishop Milingo discussed earlier in this chapter? Much of what I have said here is not going to be looked upon favorably with some - that is quite clear and evident. What is important to understand is that wherever there is smoke, there is usually fire. Are there some out there within the Church who on the surface appear to be Christian, but in quiet are actually serving a darker power? It seems clear to me that something along those lines is happening.

Does this case have its place within some diabolical scheme? I would have to say in my opinion there is cause to believe that is true. At a minimum, the 1949 Exorcism Case should be viewed as a bookmark in history for a time that saw many changes in the faith and the ideology surrounding religion. It is possible the results from this case could have helped open the door to a cycle of events that are still upon us all today, and still at the hands of the world's largest corporation, the Roman Catholic Church. The events in 1949 clearly played a part in all of it, but exactly what part and how deep will never be truly known. Whatever the final truth may be, it is also clear this case was part of a series of events that helped usher in a new age of the diabolic. The implications of this new age affect all of us in one way or another; they could be the exact thing which has played upon many fears, some of them fanatical and some of which are very real, and these same implications could be bringing us one step closer to Armageddon. If Armageddon is truly at hand, it will be important for everyone who is living within this chaotic and diabolic world to remember the reassuring words from Pope Francis, "The presence of the devil is on the first page of the Bible, and the Bible ends as well with the presence of the devil, with the victory of God over the devil." In the end, good will triumph over evil. Amen.

This prophecy came from Mary to Veronica Lueken at Bayside, NY, from 1968 to 1995:

Satan, the evils of Satanism, only appear when sin has become a way of life, and the evil has brought an immense blanket of darkness to an area. 666, Satan in human form, is wherever darkness is. He is the prince of darkness, the father of all liars, the master of deceit. And I say, my children, the master of deceit, for he is cunning beyond all human understanding. ("Fr. Malachi Martin Affirmed")— Our Lady, November 21, 1977

Appendix

When you research a historical event, you read everything on the subject that you are able to get your hands on. We have been lucky to have Father Bishop's diary and the interviews with Father Halloran, among other types of research available on the subject matter. However, some of the things stated and written about this case have been tainted in numerous ways for numerous purposes. Some have written from a completely Roman Catholic perspective, some have written completely with Blatty's novel in mind, while others have twisted the information available for their own purposes and agendas. Whether intentionally or unintentionally, urban legends and smoke screens have been enabled, which cloud the reality of the case.

We can examine Father Bowdern for more understanding. The problem with this research angle is we are dealing with a man who, while living, felt very strongly that he needed to hide the truths surrounding this possession. We have looked at the history of the man and who he was as a person before the exorcism and the effects it had on him afterward. However, other than the fact that he felt this was the real thing, there is very little in his voice to tell the facts surrounding this case. We needed to talk to Father Bowdern. We needed him to help fill in the missing pieces, but the problem was he was no longer living. We decided there was no other choice but to make a very controversial move and try to communicate with Father Bowdern in death. In order to do this, we gathered the Ovilus (ghost box) and an electronic voice phenomena (EVP) recorder, and we headed to Calvary Cemetery to the site where he was buried. Our intention was to speak with Father Bowdern. We had no idea we would end up communicating with the demon itself.

We heavily debated whether we would share this information publicly or not. It is very controversial in nature, and we would like you to keep that in mind when you read what follows. This portion of the book also comes with a very important warning. If you have an aversion to reading or speaking the name of the demon, you may feel the need to skip the transcript portion altogether. We are going to be presenting the name of the demon in the transcript.

What you are about to read is both shocking and revealing. The following is the transcript of the conversations we had with who we feel is the deceased Father Bowdern and who we theorize to be the demon that possessed Roland Doe. There were other personalities who were unidentifiable as well.

Calvary Cemetery Sessions

The first passage from the "Calvary Cemetery Sessions" that I would like to share with you is a conversation with a male voice that identified himself as Father Bowdern. The line of questioning regarded Roland's mother and the spiritualist aunt's money. I am not going to share the aunt's name with you in order to continue to keep my word about protecting Roland's identity for respect purposes.

5:33—Ovilus: "XXXXXXX." [this was the aunts name given] 5:34—EVP: "XXXXXXX." [this was the aunts name given again]
6:19—Steven: "Father, was it about the money?"
6:22—Ghost box: "Seven?" [male voice]
6:28—Shannon: "Seven thousand dollars?"
6:29—Ghost box: "Off." [male voice]
6:33—Steven: "Was it about the money?"
6:34—Ghost box: "Seventy." [male voice]
6:36—Steven: "Seventy thousand?"
6:38—Steven: "Did they find it?"
6:45—Ovilus: "Bills."
6:46—Ghost box: "Divide." [male voice]
6:55—Steven: "Did the mother sell her soul, Father?"
*6:59—Ghost box: "Yes, mense." *Mense means "sacrificial altar" in Latin*
7:05—Steven: "Father, did she sell her son?"
7:07–7:08—Ghost box: "Yes." [two female voices]
7:17—Ghost box: "Excuse me?" [male voice]
7:21—Steven: "Did she sell her son's soul, Father?"
7:22—Ghost box: "Yes." [male voice]
7:26—Steven: "Did she?"
7:32–7:33—Ghost box: "Yes." [clear male voice]

The next segment of the "Calvary Cemetery Sessions" is somewhat confusing by its subject matter. Let me share it with you first, and then we can discuss its possible meaning after you have read it.

10:24—Shannon: "Why was it blamed on Halloran?"
10:27—Shannon: "Did they claim he went crazy?
10:40—Ghost box: "Si." [male voice]
*10:45—Ghost box: "Vectus." [male voice] *Vectus means "infection" in Latin*
10:55—Steven: "Is the mother here with us?"

243

10:57—Ghost box: "Bowdern." [male voice]

There has always been some speculation to why Father Halloran was pulled from the case five days before the exorcism was completed. The whole event was taking a grueling toll on everyone involved, and I have to wonder if the reason Father Halloran was pulled off was because it was just way too much for him. That would play into the idea being presented here that he went crazy, or in this reference he maybe suffered some of sort of breakdown due to the nature of the exorcism. It also speaks of infection, which could also mean he had become ill due to his mental fatigue during the event. Notice that when speaking to us about the infection, *it* uses the Latin word *vectus*, which is also very interesting.

3:17—Shannon: "Did he get stabbed in the ear or hit in the head?"
3:18—Ghost box: "Bible." [male voice]
3:20—Steven: "He got hit in the head with a Bible?"
3:22—Ghost box: "Yes." [male voice]

The next section I would like to share with you from the "Calvary Cemetery Sessions" comes when the conversation surprisingly turns to something hidden in the basement of the church. Obviously there is no way of knowing if there is anything hidden there or not, but it is more about the way this conversation is handled which begins to paint a very clear picture of who we are speaking to. The voice begins to use anagrams to play games with its answers.

9:27—Steven: "What is in the basement of the church?"
9:31—Ghost box: "TIVI." [male voice]
9:47—Ovilus: "Letter."

Upon research, the origin of "TIVI" is as an anagram. Here are the words it can create and their meanings:

vital: life, (Latin) seventeenth-century synonyms: important, main, major, chief, spirited
vitae: feet, life (Latin)
vatic: prediction of the future
vitta: ribbon (Latin)
davit: crane-like device
vista: passage way (1600s)
vates: profit

Could there be a letter of future prediction hidden within the church? There is really no way of finding out. However, the discussion with the use of anagram is very clever. It is not so much the meaning behind what it is telling us. The delivery of the message is what is significant here. I am going to share with you one last session from another location, which I am not going to reveal due to the nature of the work there and what it houses. But the session that we held at this location helps make sense of what you have already read above. I am getting ready to name the demon that we theorize possessed Roland Doe.

Unreported Location Session

00:42—Steven: "What is the name of the demon who possessed the boy?
00:46—Ghost box: [responds in an inaudible male voice]
01:40—Ghost box: "Belial, Lucifer ... " [male voice]
02:08—Shannon: "We want to know about the demons."

02:10—Ghost box: "Demons." [male voice]
02:12—Ovilus: "Six."
02:35—Ovilus "Ten"

The demon by the name of Belial refers to a very powerful demon who has been said to be the right-hand demon to Lucifer, and some have even referred to him as the Father of Lucifer or Lucifer himself. I think it is interesting that Lucifer is named after stating the name of the demon, which could have been the start of the same type of reiteration we saw Anneliese use earlier in our text. Whatever the purpose or reason, Belial is a worthless one - a leader of armies and a trickster who likes to play games. All of a sudden the anagrams and the use of numbers to communicate begins to make sense. This is one of the higher demons in the hierarchy, and interestingly enough, it is also the demon that was named in my personal haunting case.

Do we know for sure that this was the demon? It is actually impossible to know for sure, and for that reason, I almost did not share this portion with you. We theorize this demon could have been part of the siege, partly because of the characteristics shown and partly from this communication and others. Remember the numbers 6 and 10 came up continually within the case and we have also seen them come up within the communications many times on many separate instances. Remember the riddles the demon spoke through the possessed boy. It was constantly playing games including the saying of one word, "Dominus" to force it to leave. It would appear that this trickster demon would be a good one to put on the list for consideration for sure. Even the year 49 could have been part of the demonic plan with 4+9=13. Remember the X's and 10 or 40? I think you can see easily see the point and the trend.

Location Photography

The Uncle's House
Bel-Nor, Missouri

St. Francis Xavier College Church
Saint Louis, Missouri

Cross from the old Alexian Brother's Hospital
Now Housed at:
The City Museum
Saint Louis, Missouri

Deserted Hospital Floor with Double Doors
(Possessed Priest Location)
Saint Louis, Missouri

Location of Father Bowdern's Grave
Calvary Cemetery and Mausoleum
Saint Louis, Missouri

References

Allen, Thomas B. *Possessed: The True Story of an Exorcism.* New York: Doubleday, 1993.

Barillas, Martin. "Interview with Exorcist Jose Antonio Fortea." *Spero News.* July 29, 2007, http://www. speroforum.com/a/10469/Interview-with-exorcist -Jose-Antonio-Fortea#.V4keXUXkB7M.

Box Office Mojo. "All Time Box Office: Adjusted for Ticket Price Inflation." Accessed August 2015, http://wwwboxofficemojo.com/alltime/adjusted.htm
.
Brown, Michael. "An Interview with the Priest Involved in the Case Behind *The Exorcist*." *Spirit Daily*. Accessed July 2015, http://www.spiritdaily.net/Halloran.htm.

Carrithers, Michael. *The Buddha: A Very Short Introduction*. Oxford: Oxford University Press, 1983.

"Case Study." Father Raymond Bishop's diary. 1949.

Cornelius, J. Edward. *Aleister Crowley and the Ouija Board*. Los Angeles: Feral House, 2005.

Crowley, Aleister. *Magick: Liber Aba, Book Four*. York Beach, ME: S. Weiser, 1998.

Crowley, Aleister. *Magick in Theory and Practice*. New York: Dover Publications, 1976.

Cull, Nick. "The Exorcist." *History Today*. 50 (5), 2000, http://www.historytoday.com/nick-cull/exorcist.

Fay, Monsignor William P. "The Real Presence of Jesus Christ in the Sacrament of the Eucharist: Basic Questions and Answers." *United States Conference of Catholic Bishops*. 2001. Accessed July 2015, http://www .usccb.org/prayer-and-worship/the-mass/order-of -mass/liturgy-of-the-eucharist/the-real-presence-of -jesus-christ-in-the-sacrament-of-the-eucharist-basic -questions-and-answers.cfm.

Fitzgerald, F. Scott. *The Great Gatsby*. Raleigh, NC: Hayes Barton Press, 1925.

Fortea, Fr. Jose Antonio and LeBlanc, Lawrence. *Anneliese Michel: A True Story of a Case of Demonic Possession*. Amazon Digital Services, Kindle-only edition. 2012.

"Fr. Malachi Martin Affirmed: Satanism Has Been Practiced in the Vatican." *These Last Days News*. August 10, 2015, http://www.tldm.org/news/martin.htm.

Garrison, Chad. "Hell of a House." *Riverfront Times*. October 26, 2005, http://www.riverfronttimes.com /stlouis/hell-of-a-house/Content?oid=2491650.

Henrie, Marie. "Malachi Martin — Satan Enthroned in Vatican?" *Henrymakow.com*. February 27, 2010, http:// www.henrymakow.com/malachi_martin_—.html.

Holweck, Frederick. "St. Michael the Archangel." The Catholic Encyclopedia. Vol. 10. New York:

Robert Appleton Company, 1911. 7 Sept. 2016
<http://www. newadvent.org/cathen/10275b.htm>.
The Holy Bible, King James Version. New York:
American Bible Society, 1999.

"How the Archangel Michael intervened in the case
behind 'The Exorcist,'" *Spirit Daily*. Accessed July
2015,
http://www.spiritdaily.net/michaelexorcist.htm.

Jackson, Wayne. "Demons: Ancient Superstition or
Historical Reality?" *Apologetics Press*. 1998.
Accessed June 2015,
http://www.apologeticspress.org/apcontent
.aspx?category=11&article=120.

Jenkins, Father Joe. "An Exorcism Story." *Blessed
Magazine*. December/January, 2014 Issue. Page 31-
33, https://
References 253
254 References

issuu.com/blessedmagazine/docs/blessed_magazine
_christmas_issue.

Kent, William. "Demons." *The Catholic
Encyclopedia*. Vol. 4. New York: Robert Appleton
Company, 1908. Accessed June 2015,
http://www.newadvent.org /cathen/04710a.htm.

Levi, Eliphas. *The Key of the Mysteries*.
Altenmünster: Jazzybee Verlag, 2014.

Lovgren, Stefan. "Judas Was 'Demon' After All,
New Gospel Reading Claims." *National
Geographic News*. December 21, 2007,
http://news.nationalgeographic.com/news/2007/12/0
71221-gospel-judas.html.

Manguel, Alberto. "It Takes All Kinds; Faust: The Deal Maker" *New York Times*. October 17, 1999, http:// www.nytimes.com/1999/10/17/magazine/it-takes-all -kinds-faust-the-deal-maker.html.

Marco, Meghann. *Field Guide to the Apocalypse*. New York: Simon Spotlight Entertainment, 2005.

Martin, Malachi. *The Jesuits: The Society of Jesus and the Betrayal of the Roman Catholic Church*. New York: Simon & Schuster, 1988.
———. *Hostage to the Devil: The Possession and Exorcism of Five Contemporary Americans*. San Francisco: HarperCollins Press, 1992.

———. *The Keys of This Blood*. New York: Simon & Schuster: 1991.

Mayes, Benjamin. *Quotes and Paraphrases from Lutheran Pastoral Handbooks of the 16th and 17th Centuries on the Topic of Demon Possession*. Accessed August 2015, http://www.angelfire.com/ny4/djw/lutherantheology .demonpossession.html.

McGonigle, Pat. "Pat Recalls Spooky Phone Call On 'Exorcist' Anniversary." *KSDK.com*. June 19, 2013,http://mocux.ksdk.com/story/news/2013/10/20 /3122193/.

McRobbie, Linda Rodriguez. "The Strange and Mysterious History of the Ouija Board." *Smithsonian.com*. October 27, 2013, http://www.smithsonianmag.com/history /the-strange-and-mysterious-history-of-the-ouija -board-5860627/.

"Meaning of Numbers in the Bible: The Number 40," *The Bible Study Site*. Accessed July 2015, http://www .biblestudy.org/bibleref/meaning-of-numbers-in -bible/40.html.

"Occultist Worship Numbers," *The Cutting Edge*, accessed July 2015,http://www.cuttingedge.org/pages/seminar2/NUMBERS.htm.
References 255

"Pastor-Elder Handbook," The Lutheran Church—Missouri Synod, Central Illinois Disctrict, 2012, http://www.cidlcms.org/PastorElderHandbook2012.pdf.

Peck, M. Scott. *People of the Lie*. New York: Touchstone: 1998.

"Pope: Guard Against Deceit of the Devil." *Vatican Radio*. October 11, 2013. http://en.radiovaticana.va/storico/2013/10/11/pope_guard _against_deceit_of_the_devil/en1-736378.

"Quotes from Saint Pope John Paul II," *Catholicwarfare. com*. Accessed July 2015, catholicwarfare.com.

Rayner, Mark A. *The Fridgularity.* Monkeyjoy Press: 2012.

"Satanism in the Vatican." *Hope of Israel Ministries*. Accessed August 2015, http://www.hope-of-israel.org /vaticansatan.html.
Saunders, Father William P. "What is a Blessing?" Eternal Word Television Network. Accessed August 2015,
http://www.ewtn.com/library/ANSWERS /WHATBLES.htm.

Schneible, Ann. "Practical Help for the Demon-Possessed: Vatican Rolls Out New Exorcism

Course." *Catholic News Agency.* April 10, 2015,
http://www.catholicnewsagency.
com/news/practical-help-for-the-demon-possessed -
vatican-rolls-out-new-exorcism-course-36248/.

Shelley, Marshall. "Could Demons Possess me?"
Christianity Today. Accessed July 2015,
http://www.christianitytoday
.com/iyf/advice/faithqa/could-demons-possess-me.
html.

St. Clair, David. *Child Possessed: A Chilling Story
of Possession and Exorcism.* London, Corgi: 1979.

"St. Michael the Archangel." *Catholic Harbor of
Faith and Morals.* Accessed July 2015,
http://www.newadvent .org/cathen/10275b.htm.
Squires, Nick. "Chief Exorcist Says Devil Is in
Vatican." *The Telegraph.* March 11, 2010,
http://www.telegraph
.co.uk/news/worldnews/europe/vaticancityandholys
ee /7416458/Chief-exorcist-says-Devil-is-in-
Vatican.html.

"The Tetrad 4," *Their Occult Power and Mystic
Virtues.* Accessed June 2015, http://www.sacred-
texts.com/eso /nop/nop11.htm.

Walker, Jade. "Rev. Walter H Halloran." *The Blog
of Death.* March 8, 2005.
http://www.blogofdeath.com/2005/03 /08/rev-
walter-h-halloran/.

Zaimov, Stoyan. "Pope Francis Warns of 'Sickness'
of Greed, Lust for Power, 'Spiritual Alzheimer' at
the Vatican in Christmas Speech." *Christian Post.*
December 23, 2014,
http://www.christianpost.com/news/pope-francis -
warns-of-sickness-of-greed-lust-for-power-spiritual

-alzheimer-at-the-vatican-in-christmas-speech-131575/.

To contact Steven LaChance
steven@stevenlachance.com

Lightning Source UK Ltd.
Milton Keynes UK
UKHW021845091122
411907UK00013B/1872